PONDMASTER

A practical guide to

# POND PLANTS

## AND THEIR CULTIVATION

DEREK LAMBERT

INTERPET PUBLISHING

## Author

**Derek Lambert** has been a passionate pondkeeper for over 30 years. He has always had at least one pond in his garden and has grown and propagated a wide range of pond plants. He currently has a wildlife pond. Derek is Editor of *Today's Fishkeeper* and has written many books on ponds and aquarium fish, as well as taking part in a variety of TV and radio programmes.

ISBN: 1-84286-062-3

### Credits
Created and designed: Ideas into Print,
New Ash Green, Kent DA3 8JD, England.
Production management: Consortium, Poslingford,
Suffolk CO10 8RA, England.
Print production: Sino Publishing House Ltd., Hong Kong.
Printed and bound in China.

*Below:* Marginal and moisture-loving plants are clearly flourishing around this pond. Some, such as the pink-flowered knotweed (Persicaria bistorta), *need to be kept in check to stop them taking over.*

# Contents

A large garden pond with healthy plants under, on and around the water surface.

# Improving on nature

In the last decade there has been an explosion of interest in ponds and water gardening, and millions of new ponds have been installed all over the world. For many amphibians, such as frogs, toads and newts, this has meant the difference between survival and extinction, because while all these new garden ponds were being created, many natural ponds were drained and filled in. So not only are gardeners enhancing their surroundings, they are also playing an essential part in conserving wildlife for future generations.

The plants that surround and live in the pond play a vital role in its ecosystem. Species range from moisture-loving plants that would normally be found 30cm (12in) or more away from the edge, through the marginals, which have their roots and part of their stems underwater, to true aquatic plants. Each group contains plants that are happy in more than one environment. This means that many moisture-loving plants can live partially submerged for periods of time, and marginals can tolerate drier conditions. They have to do this in the wild, because ponds and rivers tend to rise and fall depending upon rainfall.

The selection of pond plants offered for sale has also increased dramatically and it is now possible to create a pond full of colour and interest all year round. Whether you are experimenting with colour themes, a Japanese-style garden or a wildlife pond, you will need specific plants to create the desired effect. But whatever type of effect you are trying to create with your pond, remember that this is not a truly natural environment. If left to their own devices for any length of time, the plants will become overgrown and often deteriorate. Some will self-seed and spread far and wide. Others will be swamped by the more vigorous types and die off. A few years down the line your careful design will have disappeared and the impression will be one of neglect. So think of your pond as another part of the garden in need of weeding and general maintenance on a regular basis and give it a general overhaul every spring and autumn. All the hard work will be worth it; a well-designed and maintained pond will soon become the principal focal point in any garden.

# Choosing plants for your pond

Once your pond has been installed you can set about buying some plants for it. With such a large array to choose from it can be difficult to know where to start. For this reason it is often better to start by drawing a planting plan, so you have a better idea of which plants you are going to need to fill each area of the pond. There are four distinct areas that need stocking: the pond surround, which should be planted with normal garden plants in keeping with the style of pond you have decided to create; the bog garden area, where those plants that like moist soil will grow; marginal shelves, which are completely submersed; and finally deep water areas. There is a selection of plants for each area and you should make a list of those you intend to buy.

**Right:** Water lilies are the most popular plants with floating leaves. They produce a superb variety of flowers over a long period. They provide shelter for fish and help prevent the water turning green by providing some shade.

**Above:** Sweet flag (Acorus calamus) grows in the marginal zone. These plants need their roots in water and produce leaves and flowers above the surface. They form a link between the dry land and the watery depths.

**Left:** In the damp soil around the pond plants such as these candelabra primulas will flourish. They need plenty of moisture but also air in the soil as well.

# The planting zones of a pond

Bog garden plants are grown around the edge of the pond in moist but not waterlogged soil.

Marginals are usually grown in containers positioned on a shelf with up to 30cm (12in) of water above them.

Floating-leaved plants in containers on the pond bottom send up stems with leaves that create shade at the surface. Many have attractive flowers.

Floating plants also provide shade and trailing roots. Some species can be invasive and completely cover the surface.

Water lilies are floating-leaved plants and the real stars of the pond. Keep them clear of fountains and waterfalls, since they dislike water movement.

**Below:** The submerged plant zone of a pond tends to look like a green mass just under the surface. Despite this lack of aesthetic appeal, it is one of the most important planting areas because these plants help purify the water and reduce green water and blanketweed problems.

Submerged aquatic plants provide a natural filtration system for the pond. They are usually positioned in the deepest part of a pond and develop into large clumps that provide cover for fish fry and insects. Ideally, choose a spot where they will receive plenty of light.

9

Once you have prepared your planting plan and drawn up a list of the plants you need, you can start visiting garden centres and aquatic plant dealers. You will probably buy your plants in batches, partly to spread the cost, but also because you are unlikely to find all the plants you want in one outlet.

Choose your plants with care. Whatever their size, beware of cheap offers. All too often these are either inferior varieties, starved, checked, diseased or very young plants. Paying a fair price for really good plants is an investment that will grow in value year by year.

### Stocking levels

Plant stocking levels will vary depending on the type of pond you have created. You must also take into account the amount of light and how much water movement there is going to be in any particular area. For example, if you have a passion for water lilies and want to grow as many as possible, then it is theoretically possible to cover your pond with water lily leaves. The problem with this is that some of the pond may have too much water movement, which water lilies do not like. Secondly, there may not be sufficient light for them to flower well, and finally, the abundance of water lily foliage will prevent light reaching any oxygenators growing below the water surface. These plants play a vital role in maintaining the natural balance of your pond.

Although there are no hard and fast rules about how many plants you can have in a pond, the ideal seems to be that one-third of the deep water surface area should be covered in floating-leaved

plants, such as water lilies. Another third can be left open, while the final third will have oxygenators growing in containers on the pond bottom. In wildlife ponds where no fish are to be kept, it really does not matter if little open water remains, although you will want some clear areas so that you can see any amphibians or other wildlife under water. Formal ponds tend to look better when the visible planting is kept to a minimum, but you should increase the number of oxygenators to compensate for the reduced number of other plants.

In the shallow water areas where marginals are growing you can place as many containers as you have room for. It is a good idea to have clusters of the same plant, rather than single specimens dotted here and there. This can be achieved either by putting several plants of the same species together

**Above:** *About one-third of the surface should be covered with floating-leaved plants, as shown in this well-stocked pond featuring several varieties of colourful water lilies.*

**Left:** *Always read up on a plant before buying. Many plant labels have only very limited information or skim over problems such as how invasive a plant may be. Terms such as 'vigorous' or 'fast-growing' often mean that the plant can become a rampant weed!*

in one container or by placing several containers next to each other. Mixed plantings in containers rarely work well in the long term because the most vigorous species soon smother the slow-growing varieties. For this reason, buy individual plants grown in a container on their own, rather than a mixed container already planted up.

In the bog garden area you have a large selection of plants to choose from. Many of them can be invasive, so you may have to grow them in containers sunk into the waterlogged soil. A dressing of bark chips will disguise the tops of the containers. In the area closest to the water, try to select plants that will grow over the edge of the pond. Creeping Jenny (Lysimachia nummularia) and water forget-me-

*Below: A beautiful pond is not created by just the plants in the pond, but by the whole environment. Marginals and moisture-loving plants are important, as are those planted in garden soil around the edge.*

not (Myosotis scorpioides) are particularly good for this and will soon form a clump that grows right down into the water.

In the area surrounding the pond there should be sufficient plants to create an attractive display but not so many that they are cramped and have little or no room for growth. Once again, always plant in groups of a species, rather than introduce the odd individual here and there. Around a formal pond or one that is part of a patio, you can use containers filled with annual plants creating a display that changes each year. Alternatively, each container can be stocked with permanent specimen plants. Small trees such as *Acer palmatum* look particularly good in this situation.

### Planting up the pond – first phase
Start by planting up two principal areas: the deep-water area and the space around the pond. Most important of all are the deep-water species – water

*Above: Oxygenators should be planted as early as possible in a new pond's life. These should be grown in containers and carefully lowered into position.*

lilies, floating-leaved plants and oxygenators – and you can buy these as soon as all danger of frost has passed. Floating-leaved plants and water lilies are usually sold as container-grown, and provided they do not look overgrown you can place them directly in the pond. Remove any damaged leaves first.

Oxygenators are usually sold in bunches. Separate these out and plant each stem into a container. Depending on the size of the container, it may hold three or four stems or the whole bunch. Spacing them out this way creates a large thicket of plants that will receive enough light and nutrients for healthy growth.

The other area to plant up at an early stage is the one around the pond that features large plants that will take a long time to achieve a mature look. Many shrubs take a few years to establish, particularly if you start with small plants.

### Planting up the pond – second phase
Once the main structure is in place, you can buy the rest of the plants. Today, marginals for the pond are almost always sold as container-grown plants and all you need to do is trim off any dead or damaged leaves and stems before planting them. If roots are showing, you may have to repot the plant into a bigger container. You will have to do this in any case if you want to make up large containers each holding three or four plants.

The bog garden comes next. Once again, buy the larger, slower-growing plants first and then add in the fast-growing species. Always select well-grown plants with plenty of new shoots and a good root development. Never buy plants in full flower, as these are usually the most expensive. A month later, they are usually sold off at a more reasonable price because after flowering they look untidy!

In many ways, a wildlife pond is much more difficult to create than a simple ornamental pond. This is because you are trying to produce something that not only looks good, but will also become a natural home for a range of animals and plants that live in the surrounding countryside. You must take into account practical matters, such as how animals can enter and leave the pond. Likewise, you must provide winter hibernation habitats and plenty of groundcover around the pond. Consider all these factors before you even start to build the pond.

How animals can enter and leave the pond is very important. In most ornamental ponds there is a gap between the water surface and the paved edging.

*Below: Frogs and other amphibians need to be able to climb in and out of a pond with ease. This frog has a ramp to climb out of its duckweed-filled pond.*

Newts can climb up an almost vertical surface like this without too much trouble, but many other animals cannot. Hedgehogs and other mammals can, and do, drown in a pond. Birds cannot come and bathe if there is no shallow water. To solve this problem you need to incorporate a shallow water area. At its most simple, this can be a flat stone placed on an upturned flowerpot resting on a planting shelf. Ideally, and particularly if the pond is made with a butyl liner, you should create an area that slopes gently down into the water from dry land. Use stones to disguise the exposed liner or cover it with soil that is held back from the deeper water area of the pond by a raised lip. Introduce low-growing, marginal, groundcover plants into this area and it will soon become a haven for fish fry.

A rockery next to a wildlife pond will provide plenty of places for frogs and toads to hibernate. A pile of old logs and leaves will be home to all manner of wildlife. If larger shrubs are grown around the pond area, allow the leaves to remain where they fall in the autumn.

Be sure to include moisture-loving plants in the planting scheme of a wildlife pond. Normally these are grown in planting baskets around the pond edge, but for a wildlife pond this area should extend some distance around the sides and behind the pond. This is best done by creating a separate bed that will remain waterlogged all year round. To create this, dig out 45cm (18in) of soil and place some plastic sheeting or pond liner in it. Puncture the bottom every 15cm (6in) with a garden fork and make sure the sheeting hangs over the edge of the excavation.

## Helpful edges

*A bog garden is a good edging for a wildlife pond, with cover for amphibians and other creatures.*

*A flat stone on a plant pot creates a little island to help amphibians enter and leave the pond.*

Replace the original soil and dig in several bags of well-rotted manure. Before planting up, make sure the soil is thoroughly waterlogged by running a hose over the area. Always water this bed during prolonged dry spells.

Trees and shrubs nearby provide another habitat that wildlife will appreciate. Similarly, you can create a wildflower meadow next to one edge of the pond. It need not be very large, but it will encourage all sorts of insects and wildlife into the area. You can buy special packs of seed mixture to create these meadows.

Never forget the most important part of this habitat – the water. Large clumps of submerged plants will help prevent algae getting a grip and will become a natural spawning ground for fish and amphibians. They are also the home of huge numbers of insect larvae. This is where you will find dragonfly larvae hunting for small fish and tadpoles.

Your choice of fish will also make a difference to how much wildlife will take up residence in your pond. Small native fish are the best choice; koi and other large fish are not suitable for this type of pond.

**Above:** *This is a male emperor dragonfly. Once established, they will skim over the pond surface during the summer months. As a nymph, they live under water in the pond feeding on smaller insects and fish fry.*

# A wildlife bog garden

Lobelia cardinalis    Trollius europaeus

*There are many beautiful moisture-loving plants that can be used around a wildlife pond. By choosing carefully, you can have plants in bloom for most of the year.*

*Foliage plants provide cover for amphibians and other wildlife. Hostas are ideal but are prone to slug and snail attack. In a wildlife pond, you must accept that some leaves will be nibbled. After all, the pond is there for the animals it will attract into your garden, as well as for how attractive it looks to you.*

*Scented flowers attract insects. Butterflies are welcome and will be more prolific if plants their caterpillars eat grow in the bog garden or nearby.*

*Add well-rotted manure to the soil to help retain moisture.*

*Gravel layer*

*Perforated pond liner*

*Use stones to provide a neat yet natural-looking boundary between the bog garden and the pond. Echo this theme by placing a few of the same stones in the bog garden area.*

*Water lilies and other floating-leaved plants provide a hopping off point for frogs and other amphibians. They also provide a landing site for insects that lay their eggs in the water.*

# Colour-themed ponds – blue and white

Many gardeners are attracted to the idea of a colour-themed garden or area within their garden. Single-coloured flowerbeds are easy to create with the correct combination of planting. Similarly, it is perfectly possible to introduce a colour theme into your pond area. At its most dramatic, it will include the paving and other ornaments around the pond area. With the huge selection of coloured paving, wood and pottery available at most garden centres, the possibilities are endless. This sort of idea works particularly well in a formal setting; for a more informal pond, confine the colour theming to the planting scheme.

Some of the best ideas for themed gardens appear at garden shows. A visit to such a show or an evening watching the televised version of them will leave you brimming with ideas. It is worth involving all the family in features of this kind, since they are not to everyone's taste and a garden has to be enjoyed by all the people who use it, not just the creator.

*Below: The Siberian flag is a beardless iris that grows from 60-120cm (2-4ft). Two or three blue-purple flowers are carried on a branched stem. This one is* Iris sibirica *'Ewen'.*

## Plants for a blue planting scheme

*Eichhornia crassipes*
*Iris laevigata* 'Variegata'
*Iris sibirica* 'Ewen'
*Iris versicolor*
*Myosotis scorpioides*
*Pontederia cordata*
    *Primula* 'Super giants series – blue'
    *Veronica beccabunga*

### Water lilies

No hardy water lilies are available with blue flowers, but you could use tropical varieties (such as those listed here) during the summer and house them in frost-free conditions during the cold winter period.

| Small | 'Margaret Mary' |
| Medium | 'Blue Beauty' |
| Large | *Nymphaea capensis* |

*Left: Pickerel weed* (Pontederia cordata) *has deep green, heart-shaped, glossy leaves. It bears blue-purple flower spikes in late summer and early autumn.*

*Right: With fragrant, blue-purple flowers, 'Director G. T. Moore' is considered one of the deepest 'true blue' tropical water lilies.*

## Plants for a white planting scheme

Alisma plantago-aquatica
Aponogeton distachyos
Astilbe 'Irrlicht'
Calla palustris
Caltha leptosepala
Hydrocharis morsus-ranae
Lysichiton camtschatcensis
Menyanthes trifoliata
Primula 'Craddock White'
Sagittaria latifolia
Sagittaria sagittifolia 'Flore Pleno'
Saururus cernuus
Stratiotes aloides
Trapa natans
Zantedeschia aethiopica

### Water lilies

| | |
|---|---|
| Small | N. odorata minor |
| Medium | 'Gonnère' |
| | 'Virginalis' |
| Large | Nymphaea alba |
| | 'Marliacea Albida' |

'Gonnère' carries double white flowers measuring 15-20cm (6-8in) across.

**Below:** Aponogeton distachyos (water hawthorn) flowers from early summer to mid-autumn, and even later in mild years. Pure white flowers pale to cream and become dark green when they fade.

**Left:** Zantedeschia aethiopica *(arum lily) reaches 30-90cm (12-36in). The long stems are topped by white spathes 15-23cm (6-9in) long, with a bright yellow spadex. The flowers appear from early spring to early summer.*

**Above:** Nymphaea *'Gonnère' is also known as snowball because the young flowers have tightly packed petals formed in a globular shape. It does not have too large a leaf spread and is classed as a medium plant.*

# Colour-themed ponds – yellow and red

**Below:** Lysichiton americanus *(skunk cabbage)* has deep golden-yellow flowers borne on rubbery white stems in mid-spring. It has very large, bright green leaves up to 90cm (36in) tall that emerge after the flowers fade.

**Right:** 'Texas Dawn' is a beautiful bright yellow water lily with red specks on its leaves. It is really only suitable for larger ponds. For a medium-sized pond, try 'Sunrise', which has beautiful yellow curved petals. For the small pond, 'Pygmaea Helvola' would be an ideal choice.

**Above:** Trollius europaeus *(globe flower)* grows to 30-45cm (12-18in). This one has flowers of a rich, golden yellow. There are many varieties of this hardy plant; this one is one of the earliest to flower.

## Plants for a yellow planting scheme

Caltha palustris
Caltha palustris 'Flore Pleno'
Carex riparia 'Bowles' Golden'
Cotula coronopifolia
Iris pseudacorus
Lysichiton americanus
Lysimachia nummularia
Mimulus luteus
Nuphar lutea
Nymphoides peltata
Orontium aquaticum

Primula elatior
Primula florindae
Ranunculus lingua
Trollius europaeus

### Water lilies

| Small | 'Odorata Sulphurea' |
| | 'Pygmaea Helvola' |
| Medium | 'Sunrise' |
| Large | 'Marliacea Chromatella' |
| | 'Texas Dawn' |

## Plants for a red and pink planting scheme

Astilbe x *arendsii* 'Bressingham Beauty'
Astilbe x *arendsii* 'Gertrud Brix'
Astilbe x *arendsii* 'Feuer'
Astilbe chinensis var. *pumila*
Eupatorium purpureum
Hemerocallis 'Pink Damask'
Hemerocallis 'Summer Wine'
Iris ensata 'Rose Queen'
Lychnis 'Rosea Plena'
Lythrum salicaria 'The Beacon'
Lythrum salicaria 'Robert'
Primula vialii
Primula japonica
Primula secundiflora
Schizostylis coccinea 'Grandiflora'

### Water lilies

Small      'Pygmaea Rubra'
Medium   'Froebelii'
              'James Brydon'
Large      'Escarboucle'

*Right:* Astilbes have fine cut foliage and lovely feathery plumes made up of tiny flowers. They are best grown in damp shady places. This striking variety is 'Gertrud Brix'.

*Below:* Primula vialii is quite distinctive from other primulas. Flower spikes up to 13cm (5in) high appear during the summer months on tall stems. The red buds open into small pink flowers from the bottom of the spike upwards.

*Left:* This is Nymphaea 'Froebelii', a deep red water lily ideal for the smaller pond. The deep green leaves are splashed with maroon.

Ponds, and the life they contain, are very much at the mercy of the seasons, and so too is the pond keeper. Spring, summer, autumn and winter all have jobs associated with them that will help keep the pond environment a healthy one.

**Spring** is the time when everything starts to awake again for the new season. Initially, there will be little visible sign of this with just a few new green shoots on your plants and the fish beginning to move upwards toward the surface. This is the time to think about dividing your water lilies. Most varieties need dividing every 3 to 4 years.

**Early summer** will see many of the fish in your pond start to breed. New plants can continue to be added throughout the growing season and this is the best time to introduce new fish. Summer is also a time when many plant pests will be most active. If caught early, the damage to your plants can be limited and the pest eradicated before it really gets a grip.

**Autumn** is one of the most important periods for the pondkeeper. It is vital to cut back the submerged aquatic plants. Many species die back during winter and will generate a huge amount of rotting vegetable matter that will cause water quality problems. Floating plants will often disintegrate with the first frost; remove them before this happens. Dying water lily leaves are another source of pollution and of course leaf fall from surrounding trees will add to the mess. Covering the pond with a net at this time of year makes really good sense.

**Winter** is traditionally the time pondkeepers ignore the pond. That neglect can be fatal. You need to check the pond every few days. This is the time ice will form and a small area of the surface will need to be kept clear. A small pond heater is one option. Alternatively use a rubber ball to keep a small area open. Once the pond water has frozen to 5cm (2in) thick, scoop out enough water to create an air pocket 5cm (2in) deep under the ice. Cover the hole created by the ball with a piece of sacking and the water underneath this ice/air layer should remain ice free and allow a free exchange of gases.

*Above: In autumn, many plants, such as these primulas, bear ripe seeds that you can collect and sow ready for the new season.*

*Below: Sweep snow off ice so light can reach plants beneath. They still produce oxygen when enough light reaches them.*

*Above: Summer is the time to relax by your pond.* Iris laevigata *and other marginal plants will be in full bloom.*

*Left: Colourful marsh marigolds* (Caltha palustris) *are one of the first pond plants to flower in spring.*

# The pond seasons

**Winter** is the time to check that slightly tender plants wrapped in fleece or straw still have their protective cover in place, particularly after a storm. Winter is also the ideal opportunity to take stock and plan ahead. Time spent looking through new plant catalogues is time well spent.

## Winter

A pond heater will keep a small hole open to allow oxygen to enter and carbon dioxide to leave a frozen pond.

Cut back reeds and many grasses in autumn. Remove any other dead and dying foliage.

Remove rotting leaves as soon as possible. If allowed to settle in a pond, they will produce poisonous gases and endanger the fish. Consider using a net to cover the pond.

## Autumn

Late spring is the ideal time to introduce new plants and to divide many of the established ones.

## Spring

Among the first marginals to flower are marsh marigolds (Caltha palustris) and the yellow skunk cabbage (Lysichiton americanus).

**Spring** Algae is a common problem at this time of year. Tackle green water with an ultraviolet light clarifier from early spring. Filamentous algae (blanketweed) can be more difficult. Pond plants will soon starve this algae out and you can remove the strands by hand.

The pond is at its best in early to midsummer. A wide range of flowering and foliage plants put on a superb display.

## Summer

**Summer** Early summer is the time to divide many plants and add fertiliser pellets to water lily containers. Cut back rampant growers and deadhead plants that would spread seed far and wide. Lift baskets of submerged aquatic plants and replace with cuttings. Renew half of your containers this way each year.

**Autumn** Everything winds down during autumn. Once the first frosts hit in temperate zones, all the herbaceous plants will need trimming back. Any that need some winter protection should be covered with fleece or straw to protect their crowns from the worst of the weather.

As with all other plants, those grown in and around the pond are subject to attack by pests and diseases. Fortunately, few of these are particularly damaging to the plant and most can be controlled by good management of the environment. However, pond owners have a problem not shared by other gardeners, namely that the fish and wildlife that live in and around the pond are adversely affected by

*Below: The beauty of the marsh marigold's foliage in early spring is sometimes spoiled by mildew towards the end of the year.*

chemicals used to control serious pests and outbreaks of disease. If any chemical treatments are to be used, a separate quarantine pond or holding area will be essential.

## DISEASES

**Mildew** This greyish mould occasionally attacks some marginals. It is usually associated with poor growing conditions that weaken the plant. For example, it may be planted too deep in the water or kept too dry. Make sure the plant is positioned correctly and remove any affected foliage. In severe cases, remove the plant and treat it well away from the pond with a systemic fungicide, returning the plant only when the chemical has had plenty of time to dry on the foliage. Always check the label on chemical treatments to make sure they are safe to use with fish.

## Water lily crown rot

This is probably the most deadly of all the diseases to affect water lilies. The rhizome starts to turn black and the leaves turn yellow and fall off. There is no cure so make sure you check all new water lily rhizomes for any sign of a soft, black, evil-smelling area. If you even suspect this disease, do not introduce the plant to your pond. It is infectious and will spread to any other lilies growing in the pond.

## Water lily leaf spot

In this disease, reddish brown spots appear on both the upper and lower surface of the water lily pads. These enlarge and the centre rots away. Most cases

*Above: The sausage-shaped blobs of clear jelly are the eggs of the great pond snail and are often laid on the underside of lily leaves.*

occur during warm humid spells and the only solution is to remove all affected leaves before they have a chance to pass on the infection.

## PESTS

### Aquatic snails

Above the water or under the surface, snails eat plants. The best cure is not to introduce them in the first place, but that is usually easier said than done. Check all new plants for snails, no matter how small, and search over all leaf and stem surfaces for lumps of clear jelly with little black spots in it. These are snail eggs. Miss one and your pond will have snails in it, probably forever!

## Brown china mark moth

In late summer, this moth lays its eggs on floating-leaved plants. The eggs hatch out into small caterpillars that burrow into the underside of aquatic foliage. They hibernate during winter, only to return to munch their way through numerous leaves in spring. The damage can be extensive and may leave plants open to fungal attack. The cure is simple; hunt down and remove any caterpillars you can find. In extreme cases, cut off all the surface foliage and discard it. That way you can be sure that any caterpillars have been disposed of.

## Caddis fly larvae

Caddis fly larvae feed on aquatic plants and are only a minor pest in the garden pond. However, it is their habit of creating a silky case covered in bits of stick, sand, plant leaves, etc., that can cause problems. On rare occasions, the caddis fly larva has been known to cut out a small piece of pond liner and glue it to its case. If this happens deep in the pond it can cause a serious problem, with most of the water leaking out. Apart from keeping fish, which eat this pest, there is no effective way of controlling them.

## China mark moth

The china mark moth is a close relative of the brown china mark moth, but its caterpillars burrow into the stems of plants. Once again, the only remedy is to pick them off by hand.

## Iris sawfly

Iris sawflies cause very distinctive damage to iris leaves, which can be seen straight away. The hungry blue-grey caterpillar chews a series of often large semicircular holes into the edges of iris leaves. The result is very debilitating for the plant. Control is by removal of the caterpillars when you find them. Most damage occurs during early summer and again in autumn when iris sawflies breed.

## False leaf-mining midge

This pest eats a narrow line through floating leaves. The affected areas then start to rot and the leaf dies. Use a strong jet of water to wash the midges off the leaves and into your pond, where the fish eat them.

## Water lily aphids

It is not only water lilies that are affected by water lily aphids. They will attack any aquatic plants with foliage above the water surface, leaving them disfigured and weakened. A strong jet of water will wash them off the leaves and into the water, where they are eaten. Since the adults overwinter on plum and cherry trees, it is best not to plant such trees close to a pond. Apply a winter wash on plum and cherry trees situated further away.

## Water lily beetles

Water lily beetles are some of the most difficult pests to eradicate or control in a garden pond. The beetle larvae chew a furrow across the top of the water lily leaf. The surrounding tissue dies off and eventually the whole leaf falls to pieces. Regular washing with a strong jet of water will reduce the number of pests, but once established in a garden pond with plenty of marginals (where the adults overwinter), it is almost impossible to do anything but keep the infestation to a minimum.

*Right: The larva of the iris sawfly feeds on the leaf surfaces of flag iris. The larva are easy to control, but can do plenty of damage.*

*Below: The grubs of the water lily beetle have cut meandering channels in this leaf. A severe infestation can cause the leaf to decay and become a black sloppy mess.*

Generally speaking, floating plants can be tremendously useful in a pond. They provide welcome shade for the fish, reduce the amount of light reaching the water and use up nitrates, thus reducing the likelihood of an algal bloom. Many also produce attractive flowers and have interesting leaf shapes. However, a number of them can become as much of a pest as green water and blanketweed. Duckweed and azolla are the two main offenders, although others may grow so rampantly that they become a nuisance.

Duckweed seems to sneak into any pond, however carefully you wash it off all new introductions and try to make sure it never gets a grip. In the end, however, most established ponds have a covering of this plant. Some fish do eat it; koi and other carp will help keep the growth under control, but even then it can be a pest and needs netting out every week. In a large pond, this can become a real chore.

Azolla is another invasive plant in the group. It is usually introduced as an attractive floating plant, which it certainly is. The problem arises when it covers the pond surface and builds up into a thick layer, which makes it difficult to see the fish. Furthermore, when winter comes, most of the layer dies off and starts to rot, causing serious water quality problems. Once again, control is by netting out large quantities of the plant every week.

Despite these problems, the benefits of growing some floating plants in a pond far outweigh the disadvantages. A particularly good example to try is water hyacinth *(Eichhornia crassipes)*, which

**Above:** *Water lettuce, like many other floating plants, produces plantlets on runners. Once the plantlets reach a reasonable size, they can be separated from the parent plant.*

**Left:** *The best tool for this job is a strong sharp pair of scissors. If more than one plantlet is growing on the runner, separate each one carefully to produce several independent plants.*

*Trim the severed runner close to the mother plant.*

**Left:** *Water hyacinth produce runners fairly early on in the season. Separate the plantlets by cutting the runner close to the mother plant and again near the plantlet.*

*Only divide plantlets from the mother plant when they have a good root system.*

produces attractive flowers, but there are other species of floating plant to choose from.

## Propagating floating plants

Most of the plants in this group reproduce asexually by sending out runners. These produce new plantlets every so often, which remain attached to the parent plant. Eventually, a whole carpet of plants will build up. You can propagate these plants easily throughout the growing season.

## Winter care

Since many floating plants are not hardy, it is best to remove them from the surface of the pond in cool temperate areas before there is a risk of frost. They can be overwintered in a bucket in a frost-free greenhouse or conservatory. Select smaller plants for this, so that they will have enough room in the bucket to grow. You can even keep small plants growing in a glass jar on the windowsill.

*Left: Keep potentially invasive floating plants under control by regularly scooping off the surplus with a hand net. Being rich in nitrates, these plants are ideal for adding to the compost heap.*

*Above: If allowed free rein, azolla, duckweed and some other floating plants will take over the pond and smother submerged oxygenators. For the health of your fish and other wildlife, you need to keep these plants under control. A well-maintained pond would never look like this.*

# Floating plants

## Azolla filiculoides
### Fairy moss

This small plant has mosslike green leaves during much of the summer, but turns a lovely red colour in autumn or when in full sunlight. It gradually grows into a carpet that can cover the whole pond to a considerable depth, preventing the light from reaching submerged aquatics. It can become a real pest if allowed to get out of control.

**Environment:** Azolla grows fastest in full sun, although it will still do well in full shade. It does not appreciate fast-moving water, which may cause it to break up into very small pieces. It will

tolerate temperatures down to 0°C (32°F) and may survive mild winters outdoors.

**Maximum height:** 5cm (2in)

**Maximum spread:** Indefinite

**Propagation:** None needed! Pieces will break off naturally and spread the plant around the pond.

**Winter care:** Azolla is best treated as a half-hardy pond plant in cool temperate zones, so remove a handful of it from the pond before the first frosts and overwinter it in a bucket or glass jar of water in a frost-free, well-lit place.

## Eichhornia crassipes
### Water hyacinth

Water hyacinth is one of the best floating plants to introduce into a pond. It has dark green waxy leaves with swollen air-filled stems. The roots trail down into the water, providing perfect cover for small fish and wildlife. During late summer, large hyacinth-like blue flowers are produced on spikes.

**Environment:** It will tolerate a wide range of conditions, including a shaded position. However, if you want the plant to flower, it will need a bright sunny aspect and a warm summer. Will tolerate temperatures down to 0°C (32°F).

**Maximum height and depth:** 30cm (12in)

**Maximum spread (one plant):** 25cm (10in)

**Propagation:** Propagation is by runners, which are produced prolifically during the growing season. Eventually, Eichhornia crassipes will grow into a very large carpet and in many parts of the world it has become a serious pest in natural waterways.

**Winter care:** The first frosts will kill this plant, so remove a few small plants and overwinter them in a bucket in a well-lit, frost-free place.

## ▲ Hydrocharis morsus-ranae
Frogbit

This pretty little plant looks like a miniature water lily floating on the water surface. From midsummer onwards, it produces small white flowers that stand 5cm (2in) above the water surface. It can grow rapidly, but never gets out of control in a pond.

**Environment:** Grows best in a sunny spot, but will also tolerate partial shade. Hardy to -5°C (23°F).

**Maximum height:** 5cm (2in)

**Maximum spread:** 60cm (24in)

**Propagation:** Divide the clumps at any time during the growing period. Frogbit also sets seeds that will produce new plants the following spring.

**Winter care:** In autumn the foliage begins to die back and the plant falls to the bottom of the pond. Here it will survive in the form of dormant buds until the following spring, when it sends out new shoots and floats back to the surface. In particularly cold areas, the stems can be collected in autumn and overwintered in a bucket in a cool spot.

## ▶ Pistia stratiotes
Water lettuce

This plant looks just as its common name suggests – a water lettuce. It has velvety green leaves with fine hairs all over them and produces very small greenish white flowers in the folds of the leaves in midsummer. The roots hang down as much as 30cm (12in) below the water surface and are a haven for small fish and other wildlife.

**Environment:** In temperate climates, this tropical plant may not do so well. Provide a sunny position sheltered from chill winds. It will tolerate temperatures down to 2°C (35°F).

**Maximum height:** 15cm (6in)

**Maximum spread:** Indefinite

**Propagation:** Parent plants produce runners throughout the growing season. Divide these when the plantlet is about 5cm (2in) tall and has a significant leaf rosette.

**Winter care:** Water lettuce will die as soon as the first frosts strike. Remove small plants to a frost-free greenhouse or conservatory where they will receive maximum light during the cooler months.

### Lemna minor *(Duckweed)*

This tiny plant has small green leaves with short hairlike roots. Duckweed thrives in any slow-flowing or still water. Deep shade tends to slow growth, but even then it will very quickly spread over the whole surface. Fully hardy down to -15°C (5°F). It does provide shade and some fish will eat it. Otherwise, it is an invasive weed that will smother a pond in a matter of days. Once established, you will need to scoop it off the surface by the netful every week just to keep some open water to enable you to see your fish. One to avoid if at all possible.

## Salvinia auriculata
### Floating fern

The floating fern has a horizontal main shoot from which paired, mid-green to purplish brown leaves stand up above the water surface by as much as 2.5cm (1in). The plant forms spreading colonies that eventually cover the whole water surface.

**Environment:** Prefers full sun and warm conditions. Will tolerate some water movement, but if allowed to float too close to waterfalls or fountains, the plant is likely to be broken up in the current. Hardy to 10°C (50°F).

**Maximum height:** 2.5cm (1in)

**Maximum spread:** Indefinite

**Propagation:** Side shoots break off naturally as the colony grows.

**Winter care:** This plant will not tolerate cold conditions, so move it under cover long before there is any risk of frost.

*Below:* Floating fern produces fine roots that hang down in clumps from each of the crowns. These provide an excellent refuge for fish fry and other wildlife.

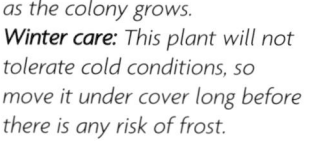

The leaves have a rippled surface.

## Stratiotes aloides
### Water soldier

This excellent plant is not so much a floating plant, since the leaves rarely float on the water surface; rather, it is a free-floating plant with no fixed root system. Looking down on it from above, it closely resembles the top of a pineapple floating in the water. The sharp, rigid, swordlike leaves may grow as long as 30cm (12in) and the whole plant may form a rosette as much as 60cm (24in) across. The root system can be extensive as well, with roots as long as 60cm (24in) hanging down to the substrate. During late summer the plant produces either single white flowers (female) or white flower clusters (male). At this time, the leaves will rise a short distance above the water surface .

**Environment:** This tolerant species does well in sun or shade, but dislikes too much water movement. During winter it sinks to the bottom of the pond. Fully hardy down to -15°C (5°F).

**Maximum height:** 30cm (12in)

**Maximum spread:** 60cm (24in)

**Propagation:** The plant sets seeds, but the quickest and easiest propagation method is to divide the numerous runners during midsummer.

**Winter care:** No special requirements.

Young water soldiers have thinner leaves than mature plants.

## ▶ Trapa natans
### Water chestnut

The water chestnut produces dark green glossy leaves on the end of swollen stems. These form rosettes that produce small white flowers during the summer months. The root system is not as extensive as that of some other floating plants, but still provides cover for fish fry and insects. After flowering, spiny fruits (nuts) are produced. These sink to the bottom of the pond and start into new growth the following spring.

**Environment:** This plant needs warm weather and a sunny position if it is to flower and produce nuts for the following season. Sadly, this rarely happens in cool temperate climates, so the plant is usually lost each year. Hardy to -5°C (23°F).

**Maximum height:** 2.5cm (1in)
**Maximum spread:** 15cm (6in)
**Propagation:** By sowing the nuts in spring.
**Winter care:** Collect any nuts from the plants in autumn before the first frost. Overwinter them in a cold but frost-free room in a bucket of water. You can leave the nuts to develop naturally on the pond bottom, but a hard winter may kill them.

In cool climates, replace the plant every year.

*Above:* Water chestnuts rarely produce nuts in cool temperate climates. A long warm sunny period is needed for the flowers to do this. The nuts have sharp spines on them and fall to the substrate during autumn. In spring, they start into growth, producing a plant that floats back to the surface of the pond.

## ▼ Utricularia vulgaris
### Greater bladderwort

This fascinating but rare plant is, in part, a carnivore. The finely divided bronze-green leaves that float just beneath the surface have bladders on them. These catch and digest microscopic animals. In late summer, yellow flowers are produced on stems standing up to 25cm (10in) above the water surface. The plant then dies back and sinks to the bottom, where it overwinters in the form of dormant buds.

**Environment:** Needs full sun and relatively little water movement. Hardy to 5°C (23°F).
**Maximum height:** 25cm (10in)
**Maximum spread:** 30cm (12in)
**Propagation:** Divide the clumps in summer.
**Winter care:** No special requirements.

*Above:* The yellow flowers of greater bladderwort are held high above the surface. The rest of the plant is a tangled mass beneath.

*Left:* Greater bladderwort is a carnivorous plant with underwater bladders that catch small animals and digest them. It is a rare plant in the trade and may be difficult to find in garden centres or aquatic outlets.

27

This group contains some of the real stars of the water garden and includes both spectacular flowering species that put on a beautiful show for a month or two and species with wonderful foliage that add interest for the entire growing season. Many can also be used to disguise the pond edge and are invaluable for providing cover so that amphibians can safely enter or leave a pond.

In the wild, marginal plants grow at pond margins, where the water level fluctuates according to rainfall and the time of year. This means that the plants are able to cope with some variation in water depth, but most have an ideal planting depth that you should take into account. At one extreme this will mean placing the crown just above the waterline, while at the other it should be well below the surface, with just the foliage showing above. Most garden centres label their plants so that you can make sure you plant them at the correct depth.

When selecting marginals, it is important to consider the vigour of each type. Some can become invasive weeds if allowed to grow unchecked. For this reason it is best to plant each species in its own planting basket, rather than allow them a free root run. Deadheading certain plants is also vital if your pond is not to be overrun by them. The water plantain *(Alisma plantago-aquatica)* is a particular problem in this respect, but there are plenty of others that seed freely. One marginal plant that seeds freely but which is never a pest is water forget-me-not *(Myosotis scorpioides)*. This pretty plant spreads by seed into any suitable habitat but is easily controlled by thinning out unwanted plants.

## Planting a marginal

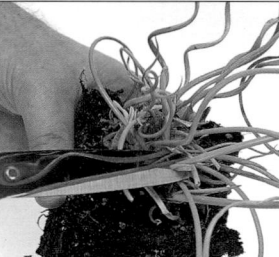

*1 Carefully remove the plant from its old container. Choose a suitable basket for repotting. Those with large holes need lining with hessian to stop soil washing away; micromesh planters (shown here) do not.*

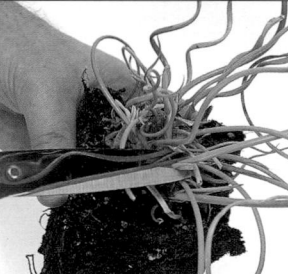

*2 Trim off any damaged stems. This is Juncus effusus 'Spiralis'. Remove any straight stems or they can take over the whole plant and you will lose the distinctive curly leaf shape this marginal plant is grown for.*

*3 Although you can plant marginals in garden soil, it is better to use aquatic planting mixture with the correct balance of nutrients. Half-fill the pot with the aquatic planting mix.*

*4 Place the plant centrally in the new container. Back fill with more planting mixture. Make sure the container is completely filled and the plant is firmly seated in its new container.*

**5** Gently firm in the planting mix so that no air pockets remain. The crown of the plant should be level with the soil, which should be about 2.5cm (1in) from the top of the pot.

**6** Using a watering can with a fine rose, thoroughly soak the mix. This will cause the soil level to fall slightly. Top up with more planting mix so that the crown is at soil level again.

**Left:** *Within a year Juncus effusus 'Spiralis' will have established itself into a sizeable clump. Its strange contorted stems provide a stark and effective contrast to most other plants at the pond margin.*

**7** Finally, add a 2.5cm (1in)-layer of aquarium gravel. Be sure to use gravel specifically sold for this purpose as some gravels contain pieces that will adversely affect the water chemistry.

**8** Water the basket again. This watering needs to be very thorough and should take a few minutes to complete. Finally, top up the gravel if it has sunk in the container.

**9** Slowly lower the container into the pond to minimise disturbance. Make sure the plant is at the correct planting depth, sits level in the water and is positioned securely on a shelf.

## Acorus calamus 'Variegatus'
Variegated sweet flag

This plant is grown for its lovely swordlike foliage rather than its small flowers. The vertically striped green-and-cream leaves are flushed rose-pink towards their base in spring. When crushed, the leaves are tangerine-scented.
**Environment:** This species does best in full sun, but will tolerate shady conditions. Hardy to -15°C (5°F).
**Planting depth:** 0–10cm (0–4in)
**Maximum height:** 90cm (36in)
**Maximum spread:** 60cm (24in)
**Propagation:** Rhizomes can be divided from late spring to late summer.
**Winter care:** Remove old or damaged leaves from this semi-evergreen plant in autumn.

*Above: The seedhead of the variegated sweet flag resembles an elongated pine cone, but this plant is mostly grown for its lovely striped foliage.*

## Alisma plantago-aquatica
Water plantain

This bright green, oval-leaved plant produces pyramidal flower spikes consisting of tiny pinkish white flowers. The spikes can grow more than 60cm (24in) tall and last for months on end in summer.
**Environment:** Prefers full sun, but will grow in most conditions. Hardy to -15°C (5°F).
**Planting depth:** 0–25cm (0–10in)
**Maximum height:** 75cm (30in)
**Maximum spread:** 45cm (18in)
**Propagation:** This species self-seeds everywhere and will soon take over a water garden if not controlled. Deadhead all flower stems as soon as they have finished flowering.
**Winter care:** Cut back the old foliage once it has died back in the autumn.

*Keep deadheading water plantains to prevent them taking over your pond.*

## Butomus umbellatus
Flowering rush

This beautiful plant has narrow, green, sword-shaped leaves that can grow 90cm (36in) tall. In summer, the flower stems rise above the leaves and produce large umbels of pink to rose-red flowers.

**Environment:** Full sun to partial shade. This plant is usually slow-growing and may take several years to flower. Hardy to -15°C (5°F).

**Planting depth:** 0-15cm (0-6in)

**Maximum height:** 90cm (39in)

**Maximum spread:** 45cm (18in)

**Propagation:** Divide clumps between late spring and late summer. Storage organs called turions are also formed at the base of mature plants. Detach and plant up.

**Winter care:** Cut back foliage as it dies off during autumn.

## Calla palustris
Bog arum

The glossy, green, heart-shaped leaves of this semi-evergreen plant scramble over the ground, forming a dense mat. Brilliant white spathes are produced in spring, followed by orange or red fruits on female plants.

**Environment:** Plant in full sun or partial shade. Hardy to -15°C (5°F).

**Planting depth:** 0-20cm (0-8in)

**Maximum height:** 25cm (10in)

**Maximum spread:** 30cm (12in)

**Propagation:** Sow seeds onto saturated soil as soon as they are ripe. Alternatively, cut the rambling stems into sections – make sure each has a healthy bud – and plant them into saturated soil during late spring.

**Winter care:** This semi-evergreen plant requires no special winter care, but remove any damaged foliage in spring.

## Caltha palustris
Marsh marigold

Several varieties of this species are available. All produce deep green, rounded leaves and form spreading clumps. The true species, Caltha palustris, has single yellow flowers that cover the plant during early spring. A smaller form (about 25cm/10in total height), Caltha palustris 'Flore Pleno', has fully double yellow flowers and is commonly found in garden centres. A rarer variety to look out for from the Himalayas is Caltha palustris var. alba, which produces pure white flowers, both in early spring and during autumn.

**Environment:** Plant in moist, neutral to slightly acidic, loamy soil in full sun or partial shade. Hardy to -15°C (5°F).

**Planting depth:** 0-10cm (0-4in)

**Maximum height:** 60cm (24in)

**Maximum spread:** 45cm (18in)

**Propagation:** Divide and replant the roots shortly after flowering in the spring. Alternatively, collect ripe seeds (but not of 'Flore Pleno') in summer and replant them in waterlogged soil.

**Winter care:** The leaves tend to die off during late summer or early autumn and should be removed to stop mildew taking hold. Otherwise, this hardy vigorous plant requires no winter care.

## ▲ Cotula coronopifolia
### Brass buttons

This pretty little deciduous plant has fleshy stems with small pointed leaves. It produces buttonlike yellow flowerheads in midsummer.
**Environment:** Plant in full or partial shade. Hardy to -5°C (23°F).
**Planting depth:** 0-5cm (0-2in)
**Maximum height:** 15cm (6in)
**Maximum spread:** 30cm (12in)
**Propagation:** Although this is a shortlived perennial, it is often treated as an annual. The plants set large amounts of seed that can be collected when ripe and sown during early spring in seed trays of moist aquatic soil. Alternatively, leave them to spread naturally and remove surplus plants every year.
**Winter care:** In cool temperate zones, low winter temperatures will kill this plant, so it is a good idea to collect some seeds to sow each spring, just in case you need to replace any plants lost during the winter.

## ▼ Cyperus longus
### Sweet galingale

A native European species of grasslike plant, with dark green, ribbed leaves. During the summer, red-brown plumes develop and these last well into winter. Both the stems and roots are sweetly scented, hence the plant's common name.
**Environment:** This is a tough, invasive plant that needs to be planted in a container if it is to be kept under control. Hardy down to -15°C (5°F).
**Planting depth:** 5-45cm (2-18in)
**Maximum height:** 90cm (36in)
**Spread:** Indefinite
**Propagation:** Lift established plants in late spring and detach the young growths. These develop very quickly and will flower the following season, if not before. The plant will also self-seed, so deadheading is important to keep it under control.
**Winter care:** Cut back the old foliage in autumn or leave it in place until spring to provide cover for wildlife.

Sweet galingale is an excellent plant for a wildlife pond.

## ▲ Eriophorum angustifolium
### Cotton grass

This strange-looking plant has grasslike leaves and cottonwool-like flowers in early summer.
**Environment:** Cotton grass needs acid conditions to thrive, so mix plenty of peat into a rich soil to create the correct planting medium. Although it will spread indefinitely, it is not as invasive as many other grasslike plants. It prefers a position in full sun and is hardy down to -5°C (23°F).
**Planting depth:** 0-5cm (0-2in)
**Maximum height:** 45cm (18in)
**Spread:** Indefinite
**Propagation:** Established clumps can be divided during spring or you can try collecting ripe seed and sowing it. However, germination is often poor, so division is more often used to propagate this plant.
**Winter care:** This evergreen plant needs little winter care, although in severe winters it may require some protection.

## Glyceria maxima var. variegata
### Variegated water grass

In spring, this herbaceous perennial grass has cream-striped leaves flushed pink towards the base. It produces panicles of creamy white flowerheads above the foliage in summer.

**Environment:** This invasive plant must be grown in a container if it is to be kept under control. It prefers full sun and is hardy down to -15°C (5°F).

**Planting depth:** 0–30cm (0–12in)

**Maximum height:** 120cm (48in)

**Spread:** Indefinite

**Propagation:** This is an easy plant to propagate. It can be divided in early spring, or you can sow ripe seeds during late summer.

**Winter care:** Cut back dead foliage in early winter or leave it in place until spring to provide cover for wildlife.

Variegated water grass is an ideal groundcover plant at the water's edge.

## Houttuynia cordata 'Chameleon'

This is a spectacular groundcover plant, with distinctive, pointed, heart-shaped, multicoloured leaves. Red, green, yellow and white patches are mixed on each leaf, apparently at random. The branching stems are produced from underground runners that spread to form large clumps. In the right conditions, this can be an invasive plant that will need regular cutting back to keep it under control. The flower cones, surrounded by four white bracts, are produced during late summer.

**Environment:** Plant in a rich moist soil in full sun or shade. Plants that receive more light tend to have more red in their leaves. Hardy to -15°C (5°F)

**Planting depth:** 0–10cm (0–4in)

**Maximum height:** 45cm (18in)

**Spread:** Indefinite

**Propagation:** Propagate by division during early spring or early autumn. Plant sections of the underground stem, each with a growing point or shoot, into 7.5cm (3in) pots of a good-quality aquatic planting mixture, which must be kept moist at all times. Once the plants have become established they can be planted in their permanent positions.

**Winter care:** No special requirements. Remove dead leaves and stalks in the autumn.

### Iris laevigata and its varieties
Asiatic water iris

Of the three main groups of irises used for the water garden, this is probably the best. The wild species produces flowers of the most beautiful blue in early summer, and if deadheaded will often produce a second flush in early autumn. The many varieties include white and pink types, as well as variations on blue, and double-flowered forms. Several variegated leaf forms are also available.
**Environment:** Plant in large groups in an open site. Irises love full sun and do best when planted in waterlogged soil with just 2.5-5cm (1-2in) of water above the rhizome. Hardy to -15°C (5°F).

**Planting depth:** 0-15cm (0-6in)
**Maximum height:** 90cm (36in)
**Spread:** Indefinite
**Propagation:** Divide the rhizomes directly after flowering. This should be done every three years to reinvigorate the plant. Seeds can also be collected and sown into waterlogged seed mixture. (Do not use aquatic potting mixture, because it does not contain sufficient nutrients for the seedlings.) A good percentage of the seeds usually germinate, although the varieties do not come true from seed.
**Winter care:** No special requirements during the winter period.

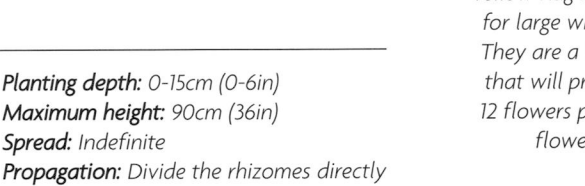

Yellow flag irises are ideal for large wildlife ponds. They are a beardless iris that will produce up to 12 flowers per branching flower stem.

### Iris pseudacorus and its varieties
Yellow flag

This very vigorous iris – a native of Europe and Asia – grows rather large for the average pond. The swordlike leaves grow up to 150cm (60in) long and lovely yellow flowers, measuring up to 9cm (3.5in) across, are produced on branching stems during early summer. There are variegated forms that are less vigorous.
**Environment:** This is a true water iris that does best when planted beside a natural pond or river. It will tolerate a wide range of conditions from full sun to partial shade. Plant in large groups for best effect. Hardy down to -15°C (5°F).
**Planting depth:** 0-45cm (0-18in), although 15-25cm (6-10in) produces the best growth rates.
**Maximum height:** 150cm (60in)
**Spread:** Indefinite
**Propagation:** Divide established plants shortly after flowering or collect seed and sow it directly into trays of waterlogged seed mixture. The varieties will not come true from seed.
**Winter care:** This very tough deciduous plant will tolerate most winters without a problem.

## Iris versicolor
### Blue flag

This American iris has blue-green, stiffly held leaves. The flowers, produced from early to midsummer, are blue with a hint of violet. A popular variety to look out for is 'Kermesina', with wine-red flowers marked with yellow.

**Environment:** *Plant in waterlogged soil in an open, sunny position. Iris versicolor is not fussy about pH, although a rich soil will produce better growth. Hardy to -15°C (5°F).*

**Planting depth:** *7.5cm (3in)*

**Maximum height in water:** *75cm (30in)*

**Spread:** *Infinite*

**Propagation:** *Divide the rhizomes shortly after flowering. Seeds can be sown into waterlogged soil in early spring. Cultivars will not come true from seeds.*

**Winter care:** *No special requirements.*

### Dividing Iris pseudacorus

*Carefully lift the whole clump using a garden fork, initially placed at least 15cm (6in) away from the plant. Wash the soil from the rootball and pull off young growths from around the edge.*

*1 Break apart the young growths so you are left with individual crowns with leaves and rootstock. If you need to use a knife, make sure it is sharp and rest the plant on a solid surface.*

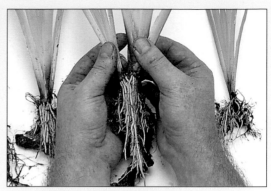

*2 Take each division and trim off the tops of the leaves to prevent wind rock. Use sharp scissors. The final leaf length should be about 15cm (6in). If the divisions are small, cut them back by two-thirds.*

*3 Plant each division, with the crown just above the soil surface. The leaves should be upright and roots well-bedded into the soil. Water after planting and top off with gravel.*

# Marginal plants

◀ **Juncus effusus 'Spiralis'**
Corkscrew rush

*There are few plants that would look perfect on the set of a science fiction movie, but this one would! Its strange, contorted, apparently lifeless stems make an untidy clump at the pondside but look very striking when planted next to more normal-looking plants. Insignificant, greenish-brown flower clusters are produced during midsummer.*

*Environment:* A moisture-loving plant that does best in full sun. It will tolerate poor, acidic soil conditions well. Since it does look so odd when planted next to other plants, it might be best to use it in a container by itself. Hardy to -15°C (5°F).

*Planting depth:* 0-7.5cm (0-3in)
*Maximum height:* 90cm (36in)
*Maximum spread:* 60cm (24in)
*Propagation:* Divide the corkscrew rush in late spring, using a sharp knife to cut through the tough rootstock. Replant the divided rootstock straightaway.
*Winter care:* From time to time, remove old foliage and any straight foliage that may appear. Otherwise, this evergreen plant will pretty much look after itself.

◀ **Lysichiton americanus**
Yellow skunk cabbage

*This much sought-after, deciduous perennial produces spectacular, bright yellow, arumlike spathes in very early spring. In fact, it is one of the first plants to flower in the water garden. The large leaves that follow act as excellent groundcover along the pond margins.*

*Environment:* This marginal plant needs a deep, rich soil if it is to thrive and should be planted in a container at least 30cm (12in) deep and 60cm (24in) across – larger if possible. Buy two to three year old specimens and plant them very carefully into their permanent position. If you damage the roots there is a strong chance they will not survive. They do well in sun or partial shade. Hardy to at least -15°C (5°F).

*Planting depth:* 0-10cm (0-4in)
*Maximum height:* 90cm (36in)
*Maximum spread:* 90cm (36in)
*Propagation:* Most plants are grown from seed and will take up to four years to start flowering. Ripe seed can be sown into waterlogged seed mixture and then pricked out into 7.5cm (3in) pots containing a rich loamy mixture. You can divide young plants that form around the base of old rhizomes.
*Winter care:* No special requirements.

## Mentha aquatica
### Water mint

There are some plants in the water garden that have everything and this is one of them. Water mint has lovely scented leaves and pretty purple flowers that attract insects throughout the summer.

**Environment:** Just like its terrestrial cousins, water mint is an extremely vigorous plant that will take over a garden if allowed to grow unchecked. Plant it in a basket or container and make sure you deadhead the plants as they finish flowering. Although this encourages more flowers, it also prevents the plant seeding itself far and wide. Water mint does well in sun or partial shade and is hardy to -5°C (23°F).

**Planting depth:** 0-15cm (0-6in)
**Maximum height:** 45cm (18in)
**Maximum spread:** Indefinite
**Propagation:** You can divide the creeping stems and rootstocks from spring through to early summer.
**Winter care:** No special requirements.

The scented leaves and pretty flowers make water mint an appealing plant for the pond.

## Menyanthes trifoliata
### Bog bean

This excellent shallow-water plant contrasts well with most upright-growing marginals because it scrambles across the ground and water surface. The three-lobed leaves are held upright, and small white flowers rise above them in spring.

**Environment:** Keep the crown of this dependable marginal plant underwater at all times. Plant it in shallow water in a basket containing aquatic mixture. Bog bean does best in full sun and is fully hardy to -15°C (5°F).

**Planting depth:** 5-10cm (2-4in)
**Maximum height:** 30cm (12in)
**Maximum spread:** Indefinite
**Propagation:** Divide overcrowded clumps or propagate by stem cuttings in spring.
**Winter care:** Remove fading flowerheads and foliage. Otherwise, this hardy perennial needs no special winter care.

▶ ## Mimulus luteus
### Yellow musk

This spreading perennial produces snapdragon-like yellow flowers (occasionally spotted with red) above hairy foliage. The mid-green leaves are rounded in shape.

**Environment:** Although this plant can tolerate having its crown underwater, it does best when grown in waterlogged soil. It prefers full sun and a rich soil, but can cope in almost all conditions. Since it will produce seeds freely and can become a nuisance, it is best grown in a container. Hardy to -5°C (23°F).

**Planting depth:** 0-15cm (0-6in)
**Maximum height:** 30cm (12in)
**Maximum spread:** 30cm (12in)
**Propagation:** Collect ripe seeds and sow them in trays of waterlogged seed mixture during spring. Alternatively, divide the overwintered rosettes in early spring.
**Winter care:** In very cold areas, treat this plant as an annual, starting the seeds in a heated greenhouse during early spring.

*Yellow musk flowers for a long period during the summer. As one flower fades, another bud further up the stem opens out.*

*Seedpods develop throughout the season. Once the seed is ripe, collect it in a paper bag, store in a dry place and sow the following spring.*

▶ ## Myosotis scorpioides
### Water forget-me-not

Just like the terrestrial forget-me-not, this pretty perennial is a real asset in any garden. The lovely blue flowers adorn clumps of light green foliage that tend to sprawl across the pond surface. More compact forms of Myosotis, such as 'Mermaid', tend to produce more flowers, but in most situations the original form is an excellent plant for disguising pond edges.

**Environment:** This vigorous native European plant does well in full sun and is particularly useful in wildlife ponds. It can be planted in any good-quality planting medium and will thrive in almost all conditions. Fully hardy down to -15°C (5°F).

**Planting depth:** 0-15cm (0-6in)
**Maximum height:** 30cm (12in)
**Maximum spread:** 60cm (24in)
**Propagation:** Divide old plants in early spring or take basal cuttings at this time. Once flowering has finished you can again take basal cuttings. Root the cuttings into a potting mix made up of 1 part sand, 1 part loam and 1 part peat and keep this permanently moist. During spring, you can also sow seeds under cover into waterlogged soil. However, these plants are unlikely to flower until the following season.
**Winter care:** Trim off old flowerheads and any stems that die back during the autumn.

*Water forget-me-not will scramble through other pondside plants, creating a lovely carpet of blue flowers.*

38

## Phalaris arundinacea
### Gardener's garters

This vigorous, evergreen, perennial grass has broad, green-and-white striped leaves. During summer it produces panicles of spikelets, containing both male and female flowers. In common with many other grasses, this very invasive species must be controlled, otherwise it will take over the pond.

**Environment:** Almost any aspect suits this grass, although it does best in partial shade. Plant it in a basket by itself and regularly check that adventitious roots are not taking hold in any containers placed close by. Hardy to -15°C (5°F).

**Planting depth:** 0-13cm (0-5in)
**Maximum height:** 90cm (36in)
**Maximum spread:** Indefinite
**Propagation:** Will self-seed all too readily, but dividing clumps during spring is the normal method of propagation.

**Winter care:** No special requirements, but cutting down the clumps in spring produces new, better-coloured growth.

Gardener's garters are best planted in a container to keep them under control.

## Pontederia cordata
### Pickerel weed

A deciduous perennial plant with glossy, lance-shaped leaves. Beautiful blue flower spikes are produced in late summer. White and pink forms can also be found, although they tend to command a premium price.

**Environment:** Plant pickerel weed in a large basket (at least 30cm/12in) and position it in full sun for best results. It takes a season to become fully established, but then it will grow well for many seasons. Hardy down to at least -15°C (5°F).

**Planting depth:** 0-15cm (0-6in)
**Maximum height:** 90cm (36in)
**Maximum spread:** 45cm (18in)
**Propagation:** Divide well-established plants when the basket becomes crowded. Do this in early spring when the plant has started actively growing. In late summer you can collect seed while it is still green and sow it in waterlogged soil.

**Winter care:** Remove dead growth in the autumn. Otherwise, no special winter care.

### Ranunculus lingua
Water buttercup, Greater spearwort

This is a tall-growing relative of the terrestrial buttercup, with all the invasive qualities of that weed. It has stout, pinkish green stems with lance-shaped leaves, and produces clusters of yellow flowers 5cm (2in) across from late spring throughout the summer. Although it is strictly speaking a deciduous perennial, it will continue to grow in all but the harshest of winters.

**Environment:** An easy, vigorous plant that will grow in most conditions. It prefers full sun but can cope with partial shade. Plant in a large basket in a rich loamy soil. Hardy to - 15°C (5°F).

**Planting depth:** 0-15cm (0-6in)
**Maximum height:** 90cm (36in)
**Maximum spread:** 30cm (12in)
**Propagation:** Divide established clumps in early spring. This plant will also self-seed; lift the seedlings when they are large enough to be handled and replant them in pots of waterlogged soil for growing on.
**Winter care:** No special requirements.

The pretty yellow flowers of water buttercups are held above the plant on wiry stems.

**Above:** The plant soon grows into a large clump and produces flowers from spring until late summer. These are much loved by insects and will attract butterflies and bees to the pond.

### Rumex sanguineus
Bloody dock

The leaves of this foliage plant are similar in shape to those of its relative, the herb sorrel, although the veins are a rich blood-red. Over a period of time, this hardy perennial will establish a sizeable clump that adds a splash of colour at the pondside.

**Environment:** Plant in full sun or partial shade in a good-quality loamy soil. To encourage new leaf growth, pinch out the flowering stems as they appear. Hardy to -5°C (23°F).

**Planting depth:** 0-5cm (0-2in)
**Maximum height:** 30cm (12in)
**Maximum spread:** 20cm (8in)
**Propagation:** Divide established clumps in spring or late summer and replant them directly into their permanent positions. If you allow the plant to flower, you can collect ripe seeds in autumn and store them in a dry, frost-free environment until spring. Sow the seeds in thin drills in damp soil. Later on, thin to 7.5cm (3in) apart before moving them to their final position.
**Winter care:** No special requirements.

**Left:** The vivid red stems and veins of the aptly named bloody dock make this an attractive foliage plant.

## Sagittaria sagittifolia
### Common arrowhead

The light-green aerial leaves are arrowhead-shaped and held well above the water surface. True aquatic leaves are also present on young plants and these are long and strap-shaped. During the summer, mature plants send up flower spikes whose compact white flowers have yellow or greenish centres.

**Environment:** Plant in a large basket (at least 15cm/6in deep) in a rich fertile soil. This species prefers full sun and a water depth of at least 15cm (6in). Fully hardy to -15°C (5°F).

**Planting depth:** 15-45cm (6-18in)
**Maximum height:** 60cm (24in)
**Maximum spread:** 60cm (24in)
**Propagation:** Divide overgrown clumps in spring or summer. Runners are also freely produced; you can separate these and pot them up.
**Winter care:** Plants produce small winter tubers (hence the alternative common name of 'duck potato') and these can be removed and planted up in the spring. The main plant is also hardy and will survive without any special winter care.

**Right:** The fully double form of the common arrowhead is known as 'Flore Pleno'. This tends to remain smaller and is considerably less invasive.

The common arrowhead has single white flowers with greenish or yellow centres.

## Saururus cernuus
### Lizard tail

This very attractive plant adds a splash of autumn colour to a pond. The heart-shaped leaves are brighter green underneath than they are on top, while the flower spikes have a distinctive arching shape and are slightly fragrant.

**Environment:** Since this can be an invasive plant, grow it in a container on its own. Use a good aquatic soil as the planting medium and position the container where the plant will receive full sun, although it will tolerate partial shade. Hardy to -15°C (5°F).

**Planting depth:** 2.5-10cm (1-4in)
**Maximum height:** 45cm (18in)
**Maximum spread:** Indefinite
**Propagation:** Propagate plants by division once they have started into growth in spring.
**Winter care:** Remove faded leaves, otherwise no special winter care is needed for this plant.

## Schoenoplectus lacustris tabernaemontani 'Zebrinus'
### Zebra rush

Certain plants are a real 'must-have' for any garden pond and this is one of them. The dramatic, quill-like stems are banded green and cream and can reach an imposing 150cm (60in) in height, although if container-grown they usually attain only 90cm (36in). In summer, flower stems bearing small brown flower tassels appear.

**Environment:** Grow in full sun in a good loamy soil. If container-grown, it should be lifted and divided every other year to help maintain the distinctive stripes. If grown in a bog garden with a free root run, the plant will creep into fresh soil, with the tired old parts tending to revert to green foliage. Hardy down to -15°C (5°F).

**Planting depth:** 0-15cm (0-6in)
**Maximum height:** 150cm (60in)
**Maximum spread:** 60cm (24in)
**Propagation:** Divide container-grown plants in spring every other year.
**Winter care:** An evergreen plant that will tolerate all but the worst winters.

Zebra rush is one of the few marginals that can tolerate brackish water conditions.

## Typha minima
### Dwarf Japanese reedmace

While all the rest of the plants in this genus are totally unsuitable for a small garden pond, this one will just about fit. The leaves are very thin and dark green, and brown, globe-shaped seedheads are formed during autumn.

**Environment:** Like all the other reedmaces, this is an invasive plant that must be planted in a container. It will grow in just about any aspect, even very exposed or shaded positions. Although not fussy about soil conditions, given a fertile planting medium it will establish faster and flower sooner. Hardy to at least -15°C (5°F).

**Planting depth:** 0-15cm (0-6in)
**Maximum height:** 45cm (18in)
**Maximum spread:** Indefinite
**Propagation:** Divide clumps during spring.
**Winter care:** Remove faded leaves during autumn.

**Left:** Typha angustifolia is a large reedmace only suitable for very large ponds or natural streams.

## ▲ Veronica beccabunga
Brooklime

A particularly useful plant for disguising pond edges or for planting in the spray of waterfalls. This low-growing, semi-evergreen creeper will spread far and wide, providing useful groundcover in a wildlife pond. It has fleshy foliage and produces small blue flowers all summer long.
**Environment:** Brooklime will thrive in almost any soil and can be invasive, so is best limited to a container. Needs full sun and shallow water, although unlike many plants it seems happy even in fast-flowing water. Hardy to -5°C (23°F).
**Planting depth:** 0-5cm (0-2in)
**Maximum height:** 15cm (6in)
**Maximum spread:** Indefinite
**Propagation:** This plant readily roots along the length of its stems. To produce more plants, just sever either side of the rooted section and a new plant will establish itself from this cutting. Take these cuttings during early summer.
**Winter care:** No special winter care is needed. However, if the plants begin to look straggly after a few seasons, cut back the stems during spring.

## ◀ Zantedeschia aethiopica
Arum lily

This is one of the most stately of all pond plants and it is a shame that it is not fully hardy. The glossy green leaves are arrow-shaped and make an attractive backdrop to the funnel-shaped, pure white, scented flowers produced on long stems throughout summer. They are some of the most elegant in the water garden and are followed by pale yellow berries.
**Environment:** Provide a good-quality, rich soil for this half-hardy plant and keep it in full sun. It can grow in moist soil and is often sold as a greenhouse plant, but will flower well if grown in a container and kept in shallow water. Generally considered hardy to only 0°C (32°F).
**Planting depth:** 0-30cm (0-12in)
**Maximum height:** 60cm (24in)
**Maximum spread:** Indefinite
**Propagation:** Divide clumps during spring.
**Winter care:** Can survive most winters outdoors, provided the crown is kept below ice level. A safer option is to remove the container to a frost-free environment for the winter. 'Crowborough' is the hardiest form and is the one to choose if the plant is to be overwintered outdoors.

A clump of arum lilies will produce a continuous succession of flowers from early summer.

# Moisture-loving plants

In the wild, moisture-loving plants are found just a little further away from the edge of the pond than marginals, or by the side of a stream. They can tolerate conditions when the soil is almost dry for a short time and most can survive the odd period of flooding. Some plants will be found on sale in the general section of a garden centre, others can be located in the aquatic area. It is even possible to find the same plant for sale in both areas, but more cheaply in the general area!

Although moisture-loving plants have to be adaptable in the wild, and some can survive in a rich, heavy garden soil that retains moisture well, to thrive long-term in the garden, they require permanently moist but not waterlogged soil. In most gardens, this will mean creating a special bed as described on page 13.

As a group the moisture-lovers include some highly desirable plants, both in terms of foliage and flowers. Ferns, hostas and sedges have very attractive foliage and can be used to really good effect, while astilbes, irises and primulas take some beating in terms of flower colour.

As with the marginals, some moisture-loving plants are invasive and must be carefully controlled. In the worst case, this may mean keeping them potted up, burying the container in the bog garden soil and disguising the top of the pot with a bark mulch. Knotweeds (*Polygonum* sp.) are a particular problem in this respect and are best left out of the bog garden altogether.

*Below:* Many moisture-loving plants, such as this lobelia, form clumps that can be easily divided to make new plants. Lift the original plant and carefully break apart the clump. Select the younger plants that have formed around the old core and plant them directly into their flowering position.

*Right:* Some moisture-loving plants are potbound when you buy them and require dividing up before planting. This geum will comfortably divide into four plants that can be potted up or planted directly into the bed. Plant the divisions about 10cm (4in) apart. As they grow they will produce a large clump that will have more impact than the single, original plant.

### Collecting seeds

The ripe seeds of many plants can be collected and sown into moist seed mix. Hosta seeds will ripen on the lower parts of the flower stem first and are easy to germinate. They will probably not look identical to the parent plant, but you may produce a new form from one of the seedlings.

## ▲ *Aruncus dioicus*
Goat's beard

This plant is far too large for most bog gardens, but if you do have the space it is well worth planting. During early summer, large (20cm/8in) fluffy flowerheads develop. At 1.8m (6ft) tall, this is an imposing plant that makes an excellent backdrop to a pond. It is not an invasive species and may take a few years to start flowering.

**Environment:** Position the plants about 75cm (30in) apart in an area of the bog garden where they will be in partial shade. They like a good deep bed with a rich soil. Fully hardy down to -15°C (5°F).

**Maximum height:** 1.8m (6ft)

**Maximum spread:** 1.2m (4ft)

**Propagation:** Divide the clumps or sow seeds during autumn.

**Winter care:** Cut the plants down to about 10cm (4in) in late autumn. Otherwise, no special care needed.

## ▶ *Astilbe*
False goat's beard

Astilbes are without doubt some of the real stars among moisture-loving plants. In spring, the new foliage is tinged a coppery red and the flower plumes, which are produced from early to midsummer, occur in a multitude of colours, from pure white to deepest red. The maximum height and spread depend on the variety.

**Environment:** These shade-loving plants do well in partial to full shade. They can tolerate a sunny position as long as the soil never dries out. They are often sold as normal garden plants, rather than in the aquatic section of a garden centre. Fully hardy down to -15°C (5°F).

**Maximum height:** 90cm (36in)

**Maximum spread:** 45cm (18in)

**Propagation:** Divide the clumps in spring or sow ripe seed during the summer. Named varieties do not come true from seed.

**Winter care:** Cut back the foliage in late autumn. Otherwise, no special care needed.

Astilbe x arendsii 'Bressingham Beauty' is one of the most popular astilbes – not surprising given its lovely pink plumes. In ideal conditions it may reach a height of 90cm (36in).

## Carex elata 'Aurea'
Bowles' golden sedge

This evergreen plant has lovely golden-yellow leaves that positively glow in the sunlight. It produces black flower spikes during summer. It is not an invasive plant.

**Environment:** This very hardy plant does well in almost any situation. It not only tolerates shade, it positively thrives in it and retains its superb colour. Fully hardy down to -15°C (5°F).

**Maximum height:** 40cm (16in)

**Maximum spread:** 15cm (6in)

**Propagation:** Divide the clumps during spring.

**Winter care:** Tidy up any damaged foliage.

## Carex pendula
Weeping sedge

This is one of the larger Carex species. During the summer it produces drooping spikes of catkin-like flowers and looks particularly good by the side of a large pond or stream.

**Environment:** Weeping sedge likes its roots to be moist all the time. It will thrive in almost any location, although it appreciates some sun. Fully hardy down to -15°C (5°F).

**Maximum height:** 120cm (48in)

**Maximum spread:** 90cm (36in)

**Propagation:** Divide the clumps in spring.

**Winter care:** No special requirements.

## Darmera peltata
Umbrella plant

This perennial has large rounded leaves and clusters of white to pale pink flowers during spring. The flowers are produced on white-haired stems before the foliage starts to grow. A very pretty plant and one well worth seeking out.

**Environment:** Grows well in sun or shade, although it needs a good, rich soil. Fully hardy down to -15°C (5°F).

**Maximum height:** 120cm (48in)

**Maximum spread:** 60cm (24in)

**Propagation:** Propagate by division in spring or by seeds in autumn or spring.

**Winter care:** Cut back the foliage in late autumn. Otherwise, no special care needed.

Umbrella plant leaves can reach 30cm (12in) across and develop vivid autumn colours, providing year-round interest.

## Eupatorium purpureum
Joe Pye weed

This native North American plant is an excellent subject for a large bog garden. It is an upright perennial that produces beautiful heads of pink-purple tubular flowers in late summer to early autumn. These attract butterflies. The stems are reddish and the oval leaves are arranged in whorls.
**Environment:** When grown in a deep bed of moist soil, it will thrive in partial shade to full sun. The plant may have problems with red spider mite or whitefly. Fully hardy down to -15°C (5°F).
**Maximum height:** 215cm (84in)
**Maximum spread:** 90cm (36in)
**Propagation:** Sow seeds in spring or divide the clumps in early spring or autumn.
**Winter care:** No special requirements.

## Filipendula purpurea
Dropwort

This upright perennial with deeply divided leaves produces large flowerheads in a lovely shade of reddish purple. Flowering starts in midsummer.
**Environment:** Dropwort does well in full sun, provided the soil is kept moist at all times. Otherwise, it is best grown in semi-shade. Fully hardy down to -15°C (5°F).
**Maximum height:** 120cm (48in)
**Maximum spread:** 60cm (24in)
**Propagation:** Propagate by seed in autumn or by division in autumn or winter.
**Winter care:** No special requirements.

## Geum rivale
Water avens

This genus of summer-flowering perennials contains one species with a number of varieties that are ideal for the bog garden. The feathery foliage is topped by bell-shaped flowers during late spring and early summer. These can be pink ('Jeannie Rose'), Orange-pink ('Leonard's Variety'), or golden yellow ('Lionel Cox') depending on variety.
**Environment:** Plant in a sunny position for best results. Geum can tolerate light shade, but will not do well in full shade. Fully hardy down to -15°C (5°F).
**Maximum height:** 45cm (18in)
**Maximum spread:** 45cm (18in)
**Propagation:** Sow seeds in autumn or divide the clumps in autumn or early spring.
**Winter care:** Leave dead foliage in place until early spring and then give the plant a general tidy-up for the new growing season. This is probably also the best time to divide the plant.

## Gunnera manicata
Prickly rhubarb

Why this plant should be available in almost every garden centre is a real mystery. Unless you have a very large area of boggy ground to grow it in, it is not a plant for the pond edge. The rhubarb-like leaves are absolutely huge (over 150cm/60in across) and the whole plant can easily top 250cm (100in) in height. In early summer, 90cm (36in)-tall flower spikes are produced. Smaller varieties are available.

**Environment:** Plant in full sun or shade. The soil must be rich, deep and always kept moist. This can cause a problem because a mature plant will require at least 22 litres (5 gallons) of water per day. Frost hardy down to -5°C (23°F).

**Maximum height:** 3m (10ft)
**Maximum spread:** 3m (10ft)

**Propagation:** Divide the crowns in early spring.

**Winter care:** Cover the crown with a thick mulch of straw to protect it from the worst of the winter weather. The old leaves can also be folded over to give it a little more protection.

*This young plant will take several years to reach its full size. The flower spike is already a prominent feature.*

## Hemerocallis sp. and its varieties
Day lilies

Day lilies are usually found in the general section of a garden centre rather than in the aquatics area. In fact, they will thrive in almost any garden soil, but in a bog garden they are in their element. During the summer months, the flowers are produced on long stems. These trumpet-shaped blooms only last a day or so, but there are dozens of buds on each stem, so the flowering period is extensive. Plenty of varieties are available, ranging from 45 to 120cm (18-48in) tall. Colours include yellow, pink, red and combinations of these colours. The straplike leaves form elegant mounds up to 60cm (24in) tall.

**Environment:** Grow in a rich soil in any aspect. Fully hardy down to -15°C (5°F).

**Maximum height:** 120cm (48in)
**Maximum spread:** 120cm (48in)

**Propagation:** Divide the clumps in autumn or spring. Seeds can also be collected when ripe and sown straightaway into pots of moist seed potting mix. They germinate the following spring and will flower two years later. These plants will still make very beautiful subjects for the water garden, but will probably not look like their parent.

**Winter care:** Tidy up the plants in autumn. Otherwise, no special winter care is needed.

*This pinky mauve day lily is aptly named 'Summer Wine'.*

## Hosta sp. and its varieties
### Plantain lilies

The leaf colour of these spectacular foliage plants ranges from green to blue and variegated forms are also available. Leaf shape and size will vary according to the variety. In the past, the flowers tended to be rather ignored, but many of the modern varieties produce beautiful blue, white or mauve flowers in midsummer. Height and spread depend on the variety.

**Environment:** An all-purpose perennial that can cope with most conditions. Ideally, it prefers full to partial shade in damp but not waterlogged conditions. The foliage is always eaten by slugs and snails, although the larger blue varieties tend to be more resistant. In the pond area it is generally not safe to use slug pellets to control the damage. Use nematode worms and other organic methods to control slug numbers and encourage as many frogs and toads as possible into your garden. Fully hardy down to -15°C (5°F).

**Maximum height:** 90cm (36in)

**Maximum spread:** 60cm (24in)

**Propagation:** Divide the clumps in early spring or autumn or sow ripe seed into moist seed potting mix. The young plants will probably not look like their parent, but you usually produce some attractive plants for your garden this way.

**Winter care:** Remove faded foliage in the autumn.

**Above:** Many of the blue-leaved hostas, such as this 'Blue Seer', are more resistant to slug and snail damage than other colour forms. The emergent leaves of all forms, however, are particularly at risk.

**Left:** Hosta 'Golden Tiara' is a smaller variety growing to about 15cm (6in) high and 30cm (12in) across. The heart-shaped leaves are beautifully set off by the lavender purple flowers. An elegant plant.

## Inula hookeri

A clump-forming perennial with lance-shaped hairy leaves and a mass of pale yellow, scented flowers in mid- to late summer. These are produced from woolly buds and have highly distinctive raylike petals. The plant is very vigorous and in the right conditions can become invasive. It will relish the moist (but well-drained) soil conditions of a bog garden.

**Environment:** Needs full sun to be seen at its best, although it will tolerate partial shade. Given the invasive nature of this plant, it is important to deadhead the flowers as they finish and regularly divide the clump to keep it to a manageable size. Fully hardy down to -15°C (5°F).

**Maximum height:** 75cm (30in)

**Maximum spread:** 75cm (30in)

**Propagation:** Divide the clump in spring or autumn or sow seeds in the spring. If allowed to seed naturally, many small plants will be produced around the base of the mature clump. These can be lifted and planted in a new area.

**Winter care:** No special requirements.

## ▼ *Iris ensata* and its varieties
### Japanese iris

This beardless Japanese iris produces stems supporting between three and fifteen flowers. The blooms can measure 7.5-15cm (3-6in) across and occur in hundreds of different forms, including doubles, bicolours, and shades of lavender, pink, purple and white. Flowering time is early to midsummer.
**Environment:** *Prefers light shade and a moist acidic soil. It dislikes waterlogged conditions in winter. Fully hardy down to -15°C (5°F).*
**Maximum height:** *90cm (36in)*
**Maximum spread:** *Indefinite but not invasive.*
**Propagation:** *Divide the clumps directly after they have flowered.*
**Winter care:** *Make sure the plant does not become waterlogged.*

*The leaves of* Iris ensata *have a prominent midrib, absent in* Iris laevigata.

*These are the stunning flowers of* Iris ensata *'Sei Shounagon'.*

## ▶ *Iris sibirica* and varieties
### Siberian flag iris

*A beardless Siberian iris that flowers from late spring to early summer. Two or three blooms measuring 5-10cm (2-4in) across are borne on each branched stem. The flowers occur in shades of blue, blue-purple or violet depending on the variety.*
**Environment:** *Prefers partial shade and moist but not waterlogged conditions. Fully hardy down to -15°C (5°F).*
**Maximum height:** *120cm (48in)*
**Maximum spread:** *Indefinite*
**Propagation:** *Divide the clumps directly after flowering. Do this regularly to maintain the plant's vigour.*
**Winter care:** *Prevent the soil from becoming over wet. No other special winter care is needed.*

*There are many beautiful varieties of the Siberian flag iris. This species does not require an acidic soil, unlike many other irises.*

## Ligularia dentata
Golden rays

The large heart-shaped leaves of this plant help smother weeds, but they are prone to attack by slugs and snails. In mid- to late summer, terminal clusters of large, daisylike, bright orange flowers are produced. There are several varieties in cultivation.

**Environment:** Prefers a moist but well-drained soil. Plant in full sun or partial shade for best results. Fully hardy down to -15°C (5°F).
**Maximum height:** 120cm (48in)
**Maximum spread:** 60cm (24in)
**Propagation:** Divide the clumps in autumn or spring.
**Winter care:** No special requirements.

## Ligularia stenocephala
Leopard plant

This plant is similar to golden rays, but the small yellow flowers are borne on erect spikes rather than wide heads. Flowering period mid- to late summer.

**Environment:** Plant in partial to full shade and in a rich moist soil. Cut down the flower stems when flowering is over and divide the clumps every three years to maintain the plants vigour. Fully hardy down to -15°C (5°F).
**Maximum height:** 150cm (60in)
**Maximum spread:** 90cm (36in)
**Propagation:** Divide the clumps in autumn or spring.
**Winter care:** No special requirements.

## Lobelia cardinalis
Cardinal flower

This clump-forming perennial is a very beautiful waterside plant that justly deserves its popularity. The lance-shaped leaves are bright green and racemes of bright scarlet-red flowers are produced in mid- to late summer. 'Queen Victoria', a variety of L. fulgens, is often sold as this plant.

**Environment:** L. cardinalis can be grown either as a bog garden plant or as a marginal. It prefers a rich soil and a bright sunny aspect. Frost hardy down to -5°C (23°F).

**Maximum height:** 90cm (36in)
**Maximum spread:** 25cm (10in)
**Propagation:** Divide the clump in spring or take cuttings during the summer months.
**Winter care:** This plant needs winter protection if it is grown in a bog garden in a cool temperate area. Cover the crown with a mulch of straw, and as an added back-up, take cuttings during the summer and keep some of these in a greenhouse or conservatory over the winter period.

# Moisture-loving plants

▶ **Lysimachia nummularia**

Creeping Jenny

This old favourite is an excellent groundcover plant that will spread over the liner and down into the water, thus blurring the edge between water and land. As well as the normal green-leaved form, there is also a bright yellow variety called 'Aurea'. Yellow flowers are produced in the leaf axils during summer.

**Environment:** Plant in any aspect (although 'Aurea' will produce green leaves in full shade) and in moist but not waterlogged soil. Fully hardy down to -15°C (5°F).

**Maximum height:** 5cm (2in)

**Maximum spread:** Indefinite

**Propagation:** Divide clumps during spring, or lift self-sown seedlings and replant them in their final position.

**Winter care:** No special requirements.

▶ **Lythrum salicaria**

Purple loosestrife

A perennial that produces racemes of four-petalled flowers from mid- to late summer. There are several varieties in cultivation, with flowers that range in colour from pink to purple and red.

**Environment:** Thrives in full sun or partial shade and in a rich moist or wet soil. Fully hardy down to -15°C (5°F).

**Maximum height:** 150cm (60in) for the wild species, but most cultivars are shorter.

**Maximum spread:** 60cm (24in)

**Propagation:** Divide the clumps in autumn. Seeds can be sown in spring, but the named varieties will not come true.

**Winter care:** No special requirements.

*The elegant flower spikes of purple loosestrife provide colour all summer long.*

52

## Osmunda regalis
### Royal fern

An elegant deciduous fern, with oval to oblong, divided lime green fronds that change to bronze at the onset of autumn. The spore-bearing fronds look very different; they are carried on a stalk and are rust-brown in colour.
**Environment:** Prefers a shaded position, although unlike most other members of this genus, *Osmunda regalis* will tolerate a sunny position. The soil must be lime-free

and kept very wet at all times. Remove any faded fronds. Fully hardy down to -15°C (5°F).
**Maximum height:** 1.8m (6ft)
**Maximum spread:** 90cm (36in)
**Propagation:** Divide the plants in autumn or winter. Spores can be sown as soon as they are ripe.
**Winter care:** In very cold areas, cover the crown with a mulch of straw.

## Matteuccia struthiopteris
### Ostrich feather fern

The idea of using ferns in garden design has really taken off in recent years and this species is one of the best for a bog garden, adding an occasional point of interest when spot-planted among flowering plants. It produces feathery green fronds that surround smaller brown fronds.
**Environment:** Grows well in semi-shade and in wet soil. Do not be misled by its rather delicate appearance; ostrich feather fern is in fact a very tough plant. Fully hardy down to -15°C (5°F).
**Maximum height:** 90cm (36in)
**Maximum spread:** 45cm (18in)
**Propagation:** Divide the plants when they become overcrowded. The best time to do this is in autumn or winter.
**Winter care:** No special requirements.

Ostrich feather ferns are so named because they resemble the feathers so beloved of Victorian ladies.

# Moisture-loving plants

## *Primula* sp. and varieties
Candelabra primula

*This group of primulas includes a number of species and varieties. All produce tubular flowers borne in tiered whorls up the stem. They vary in height from 15 to 90cm (6-36in) and are available in a range of colours. The flowering period will depend on the variety, but most forms flower from late spring to early summer.*

**Environment:** Plant in full sun or shade. Most forms prefer a rich, peaty soil that is kept moist at all times. This is particularly important when the primulas are planted in a sunny position. Most types are fully hardy down to -15°C (5°F), but some are only frost-hardy down to -5°C (23°F). Look on the care labels when you buy the plants for guidance on their frost hardiness.

**Maximum height:** 90cm (36in)
**Maximum spread:** 45cm (18in)

**Propagation:** Simply divide the clumps during the spring.

**Winter care:** Fully hardy types need no special care. Frost-hardy varieties in cold areas are best given some winter protection. You can cover them with fleece or, better still, lift the plants in autumn and keep them in a light, cool place until the following spring.

## *Primula denticulata*
Drumstick primula

*A spring-flowering primula with long, flat, oval, mid-green leaves. The flowers are produced at the top of a long flower stem and form a globe. There are lavender, white, blue and pale purple varieties.*

**Environment:** Grow in partial shade or full sun in soil that is moist but well drained. Fully hardy down to -15°C (5°F).

**Maximum height:** 60cm (24in)
**Maximum spread:** 45cm (18in)

**Propagation:** Divide the clumps in spring.

**Winter care:** No special requirements.

## Primula florindae
### Giant Himalayan cowslip

One of the largest and most vigorous of the primulas. This species has scented, bell-shaped, yellow flowers held on tall stems during summer. Some varieties have broad, lance-shaped, red-tinted leaves that are dense enough to suppress most weeds.

**Environment:** Thrives in a rich, damp peaty soil. Best planted in a shady position where it will receive some sunlight for at least part of the day. Fully hardy down to -15°C (5°F).
**Maximum height:** 120cm (48in)
**Maximum spread:** 60cm (24in)
**Propagation:** Divide the clumps during spring. Ripe seeds can also be collected and sown into moist soil.
**Winter care:** No special requirements.

Flower clusters are carried on tall stems.

## Primula vialii
### Orchard primula

This pretty plant is not seen as often as many of the other primulas, which is a shame because it does have a lot to offer. The lance-shaped leaves are a pleasant light green colour, and in late spring, long stalks topped with red and pink flower spikes arise from the centre of the plant.

**Environment:** Does best in a partially shaded spot, although it can be grown in full sun. The soil needs to be acidic, peaty and moist at all times. Frost-hardy down to -5°C ( 23°F).
**Maximum height:** 45cm (18in)
**Maximum spread:** 30cm (12in)
**Propagation:** Divide the clumps in spring.
**Winter care:** In many areas, some winter protection will be needed. Horticultural fleece available from garden centres will help protect the plants. Alternatively, grow the plants in containers and move them to a protected environment during the winter.

### Persicaria - knotweeds

The knotweeds include a number of plants that are highly invasive weeds, which can be an absolute pest in the bog garden. Persicaria bistorta 'Superba', shown here, can be a problem if allowed a free root run, so grow it in a container and deadhead the plants as the flowers finish. The pink flower spikes are produced in early summer.

## ▷ Rheum palmatum
Ornamental rhubarb

This stately foliage plant is second only to Gunnera manicata *in size and stature. The huge, deeply cut leaves form a large mass, ideal for suppressing weeds. During early summer, tall spires of creamy white, fluffy flower panicles are sent up above the leaves. These can be as tall as 2.5m (8ft). Several alternative forms are available. Just as impressive but with better colour is 'Atrosanguineum', which has red undersides to its leaves. A smaller version, 'Ace of Hearts', only grows to about 90cm (36in) and has pink flowers.*
**Environment:** *Plant in full sun or partial shade. This plant needs a deep rich soil that is kept moist at all times. Fully hardy down to -15°C (5°F).*
**Maximum height:** *2.5m (8ft)*
**Maximum spread:** *1.8m (6ft)*
**Propagation:** *Divide the crowns during early spring while they are still dormant.*
**Winter care:** *No special requirements.*

*There are several different varieties of* Rheum palmatum *in cultivation. This is the strikingly coloured 'Atrosanguineum'.*

## ▲ Rodgersia podophylla
Rodgersia

*An excellent groundcover plant that produces a large clump of horse chestnut-shaped leaves. These are tinged bronze and crinkled with veins. Fragrant plumes of small creamy white blooms are produced during midsummer.*
**Environment:** *Plant in full sun in a deep bed of neutral to acidic, humus-rich soil. Fully hardy down to -15°C (5°F).*
**Maximum height:** *90cm (36in)*
**Maximum spread:** *90cm (36in)*
**Propagation:** *Propagate by seeds in autumn or by division in spring.*
**Winter care:** *No special requirements.*

### Trollius europaeus
Globe flower

A pretty, spring-flowering perennial that forms a neat clump of deeply divided leaves. The flowers are bright yellow and held above the foliage on wiry stems. A number of other species and varieties are available.

**Environment:** Plant in a heavy, loamy soil that stays moist all year round. Under these conditions the plant produces a lusher growth of leaves and more flowers. Can be grown in full sun or partial shade. Fully hardy down to -15°C (5°F).

**Maximum height:** 60cm (24in)

**Maximum spread:** 45cm (18in)

**Propagation:** Propagate by division in early autumn or by seed in summer or autumn.

**Winter care:** No special requirements.

### Spartina pectinata 'Aureomarginata'
Variegated prairie cord grass

Grasses make an excellent backdrop to any pond and this large impressive plant has long, arching, yellow-striped leaves. In late autumn to early winter, these change colour and become orange-brown. Graceful stems of red flower spires appear above the foliage from late summer.

**Environment:** Plant in full sun in a deep, moist bed that is never allowed to dry out. Fully hardy down to -15°C (5°F).

**Maximum height:** 1.8m (6ft)

**Maximum spread:** Indefinite

**Propagation:** Divide the clumps in spring before the plant is in active growth.

**Winter care:** Remove faded leaves in early winter.

## Floating-leaved plants

Floating-leaved plants have their roots growing in the pond substrate and send up long stems to the water surface, where the leaves float. Strictly speaking, this group of pond plants includes the water lilies, but they have their own section in this book (see pages 62-69). However, with such a star in the group, the other floating-leaved plants are often overlooked by pondkeepers, yet they include some excellent plants and should be grown more widely.

All the floating-leaved plants featured here have a dual role to play in the pond. First and foremost, their leaves – and often their flowers – are very attractive. Unlike water lilies, which cannot tolerate strong water movement, several of these plants will thrive in turbulent water right next to a waterfall or fountain. In addition, they do not need as much sunlight. A water lily grown in partial shade will rarely flower, but here we have plants that will not only grow but flower well in partial shade.

The other role these plants perform is to create shaded areas underneath which pond fish can shelter. This is particularly valuable during the hot summer months, when pond fish can suffer from sunburn if no shade is provided for them. Wildlife ponds also benefit from the inclusion of floating-leaved plants because their leaves form a platform on which insects and amphibians can rest. Aquatic snails often lay their eggs underneath the leaves and baby fish can shelter between the tightly packed stems near the crowns of the floating-leaved plants.

*1 Many floating-leaved plants are propagated by runners. These are easy to divide using a sharp pair of scissors to cut the runner each side of the plantlet. Make the cut as close to the crown of the plantlet as possible without damaging it.*

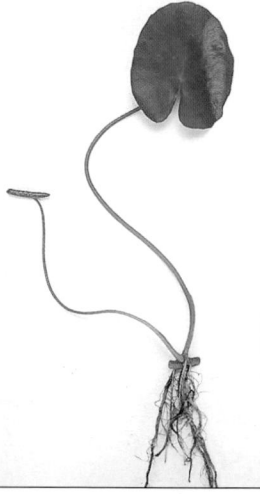

*2 Select larger plantlets for repotting and discard the very small ones. The ideal size to keep will be a plantlet with several leaves and a well-developed root system like this one. Remove any damaged leaves or roots before planting it up.*

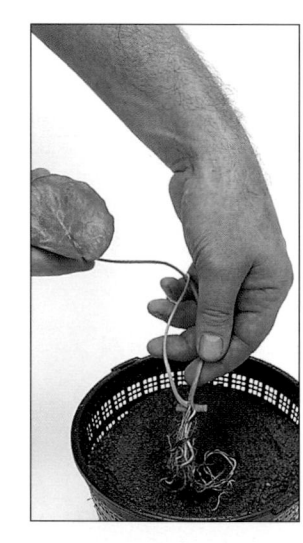

*3 When potting up, partially fill a container with aquatic soil and leave a central hole for the root system. Lower the plant into position and backfill with soil. The crown of the plant should sit just level with the soil surface. Water well with a fine rose watering can and topdress with aquarium gravel before placing the container in the pond.*

*Right:* Floating-leaved plants dominate this wildlife pond, notably a large water lily and the leaves and yellow flowers of Nuphar lutea *(spatterdock).* In fact, the pond shows signs of being overcrowded. The water lily has its leaves bunched up and sticking out of the water, which is a classic sign that it needs dividing or that the variety is too big for the pond. In the same way, the Nuphar lutea *has spread to cover most of the water surface and is really too large for this size pond. A complete overhaul is needed. The water lily should be divided and the variety checked to make sure it is suitable for the pond. The* Nuphar lutea *is probably best removed altogether and replaced with* Aponogeton distachyos *(water hawthorn).*

Although wildlife ponds often look a little overgrown, it is vital to maintain a balance and have at least half the surface clear of floating leaves.

## Aponogeton distachyos
Water hawthorn

*This is an excellent plant for a medium-sized garden pond. Its almost evergreen leaves are oblong in shape. During spring and autumn, pretty, scented white flowers are held well clear of the water surface. Deadhead plants regularly to encourage the production of more flowers.*

**Environment:** *These plants are much more tolerant of shade and water movement than water lilies and can be positioned near a fountain or waterfall, where the turbulence would upset a lily. However, they do best when grown in full sun. Hardy to -5°C (23°F).*

**Planting depth:** *30-60cm (12-24in)*

**Maximum height:** *15cm (6in)*

**Maximum spread:** *120cm (48in)*

**Propagation:** *Propagation is by division during spring, or by seed. These are produced in profusion throughout the season and can be sown into seed trays submerged under a good depth of water. Increase the water depth as the plants grow.*

**Winter care:** *This semi-evergreen plant has no special winter requirements.*

*Water hawthorn flowers look like white butterflies resting on the floating leaves.*

## Nuphar lutea
Brandy bottle, spatterdock, yellow pond lily

*This is a large floating-leaved plant with thick oval leaves. The bright yellow flowers are held well above the water surface. The creeping rootstock can be 10cm (4in) thick and may grow as long as 1.8m (6ft).*

**Environment:** *Unlike water lilies, to which it is closely related, this plant will tolerate deep flowing water and shade. It even survives in acidic water, which most lilies hate. Fully hardy down to -15°C (5°F).*

**Planting depth:** *90cm-2.5m (3-8ft)*

**Maximum height:** *15cm (6in)*

**Maximum spread:** *1.8m (6ft)*

**Propagation:** *Division in spring is possible, but since side shoots from the rhizome are rarely produced, suitable opportunities for this are few. Alternatively, collect ripe seed and sow it into pots of aquatic soil. Cover with a fine layer of gravel and submerge the pot underwater. Prick out seedlings into individual containers when they are large enough to handle.*

**Winter care:** *Remove fading leaves during autumn.*

## ▲ Nymphoides peltata
Water fringe

The 5cm (2in)-wide leaves look for all the world like miniature water lily leaves. Sadly, the pretty yellow flowers do not resemble water lilies, but are produced prolifically during the summer. By deadheading the plants you can extend the flowering season into the autumn and reduce the number of self-seeded plantlets produced. This can be an invasive species if not controlled.
**Environment:** Control this vigorous plant by growing it in a basket. It does well in shallow water in full sun and will tolerate flowing water well. Fully hardy down to -15°C (5°F).
**Planting depth:** 15-45cm (6-18in)
**Maximum height:** 7.5cm (3in)
**Maximum spread:** Indefinite
**Propagation:** Propagation is all too easy! The plant will self-seed unless deadheaded regularly and it will also send out runners. These can be detached to form new plants.
**Winter care:** No special requirements.

The leaves of water fringe resemble those of water lilies. They provide a safe haven for many insects and small fish.

## ▼ Orontium aquaticum
Golden club

The lance-shaped leaves will float or stand up above the water surface depending on the depth of water the plant is grown in. During spring, long thin flower spikes are sent up above the foliage. The ends of these are yellow while the rest is white.
**Environment:** This plant is best grown in full sun in at least 30cm (12in) of water, so that the leaves float on the water surface. Plant it in a very large container so that it will have plenty of room to grow and need not be disturbed for a long time. Fully hardy down to -15°C (5°F).
**Planting depth:** 10-45cm (4-18in)
**Maximum height:** 45cm (18in)
**Maximum spread:** 60cm (24in)
**Propagation:** Collect fresh seeds in midsummer and sow them directly into submerged pots of aquatic soil.
**Winter care:** No special requirements.

# Water lilies

Water lilies are not really considered an optional extra when it comes to a pond, but an absolute necessity! It is not only the beautiful flowers, which appear throughout the summer, that make them so desirable, but also the lovely lily pads themselves. Many have marbled patterns or are different shades of reddish green rather than plain green. They also serve a very useful purpose in providing cover for fish and cutting down on the amount of light reaching the water, thus reducing algae problems.

There are huge numbers of species and varieties to choose from, but the cheapest and most commonly available are usually the very vigorous ones that grow far too large for the average garden pond. For this reason check out the planting depth and spread of a water lily before you buy it and, ideally, select a named variety of the colour and size you want.

For the purposes of this book we have divided water lilies into three categories: small, medium and large. However, this is a rather arbitrary demarcation, since varieties cannot really be pigeon-holed so easily; water depth and lighting conditions will affect how large and vigorous a plant will grow. Also, you must bear in mind that one supplier's version of, say, a 'St Louis Gold' might not be the same as another's.

*Water lilies grow from buds, or eyes, found on the rhizome.*

*The leaves are held on long thin stems. These are brittle and easily broken in transit.*

*The root system can be quite extensive and in large varieties may become too large for one person to lift.*

*1 Water lily rootstocks, or rhizomes, may be conical or horizontal, as here. Before planting, trim back any dead areas (often found at the end furthest away from the growing tip) and check for signs of disease.*

*2 Place in a hole deep enough for the roots, with the growing tip pointing slightly upwards and towards a corner. As this type of lily grows, it will move along the basket until the growing tip is outside the container.*

*3 Lay the rest of the rhizome just level with the soil surface. Fill in the hole with aquatic potting mix and firm gently. Water well with a fine rose watering can. If necessary, add more mix to cover most of the rhizome.*

## Dividing a water lily

A water lily with a conical rhizome, as here, can be divided if it has two or more growing points. Horizontal-growing rhizomes send out side shoots, which can also be cut away to make separate plants.

**1** Once lifted from the pond, remove the water lily from its basket and wash off all the soil. This is a small plant with two distinct growing tips, and can be easily divided to make two plants.

**2** Using a sharp knife, lay the plant on a firm, level surface and cut the rhizome cleanly between the two growing points. In large plants, the rhizome can be very tough to cut.

**4** Make sure that the growing tip is still pointing slightly upwards and out of the mix. The rhizome should still be level with the soil surface and the roots covered.

**6** Only the growing tip and a little of the rhizome are visible. After about three years, the growing tip will be hanging over the side and the plant will need repotting.

**5** Using a trowel, cover the soil surface with a 2.5cm (1in) layer of aquarium gravel. Other types of gravel may contain substances harmful to fish.

**7** Give the basket a final, thorough watering to drive out any air pockets. Flattening your hands against the gravel, gently firm in the potting mix and gravel.

# Small water lilies

Small water lilies are those with a maximum spread of 60cm (24in) and need only be planted 10-25cm (4-10in) deep. They are ideal for smaller ponds and water features and provide maximum surface cover of about 0.3m² (3ft²). The leaf size varies from 2.5 to 5cm (1-2in) and the flowers are 5-10cm (2-4in) across, depending on the variety.

Plant small water lilies in a 3 or 4-litre pot. When you first put the container in the pond, raise it up on some stones so that the crown of the plant is only 10cm (4in) below the water surface. As new leaves grow up to the surface, lower the water lily basket a little each week until it is at its final planting depth.

**Left:** 'Pygmaea Alba' is the smallest of the white water lilies. It has a spread of only about 45cm (18in) and the blooms measure 2.5cm (1in) across. Bright yellow stamens set off the pure white flowers, which are produced in great numbers and held clear of the water surface. Although basically hardy, do not allow it to become frozen in ice if grown in a half-barrel water feature.

**Right:** Of the small pinks, 'Laydekeri Liliacea', with a spread of 60cm (24in), is one of the best. Its cup-shaped, pale pink blooms darken with age and have the added advantage of being scented. The leaves are spotted with reddish brown.

**Below:** *Red water lilies in this category are difficult to find, but many outlets offer 'Pygmaea Rubra'. Sadly, this is not always the plant actually sold, but if you are lucky enough to find the true plant it will have a maximum spread of 45cm (18in) and be hardy in cool temperate zones, although slow growing.*

*The star-shaped flowers of this elegant variety have prominent golden stamens.*

**Above:** *'Pygmaea Helvola' is probably the most popular of the small yellow water lilies, and justly so. All summer long, it freely produces bright yellow flowers that are held above brown speckled leaves. Maximum spread 45cm (18in).*

## Medium-sized water lilies

Medium-sized water lilies range in size up to plants with a maximum spread of 150cm (60in). They require a planting depth of between 15 and 60cm (6-24in), although most seem to do best at 45cm (18in). They produce blooms measuring 10-18cm (4-7in) across and are available in a wide range of colours. This group includes many varieties originally produced by the legendary French water lily breeder M. Joseph Bory Latour-Marliac. The first of these appeared in 1877 and was followed by an incredible number of varieties developed over a 30-year period. Sadly, his secret methods died with him in 1911 and it has only been in recent years that other breeders have started to rediscover this lost art. The result is that nearly all the varieties offered for sale at garden centres today were created over 80 years ago.

*Below:* 'James Brydon', a lovely shade of carmine red with bright orange stamens, is one of the most adaptable water lilies; it can even tolerate partial shade and still produce flowers. The leaves are tinted purple.

*Above:* The flowers of Nymphaea odorata rosea *are pale pink with yellow stamens, each bloom measuring 13cm (5in) across. It can adapt to a planting depth of 25-60cm (10-24in) and spreads to about 150cm (60in).*

**Above:** With its brilliant canary yellow flowers and bright yellow stamens, 'Sunrise' is one of the best of the yellows. Add in a flower size of over 20cm (8in) and you really have a cracker of a water lily.

**Right:** 'Marliacea Albida' has pure white blooms with yellow stamens. These can measure 15cm (6in) across and are beautifully scented. No wonder that this is probably the most popular of all the water lilies and certainly one of the most reliable.

## Large water lilies

When grown in sizeable lakes and substantial ornamental ponds, large water lilies are spectacular plants. The problem starts when people try planting them in a small garden pond. In no time at all there are leaves sticking up out of the water and the plants cease flowering. All the large water lilies require a planting depth of 38-90cm (15-36in) and will spread to over 2.5m (8ft) across. Flowers range in size from 15 to 25cm (6-10in) and are available in the full range of colours.

When looking down a plant list or around a garden centre you will see a number of water lilies marked up at a lower price than the rest. These will usually belong to the large water lily group because they are faster to grow than the smaller forms. Unless you have a very large pond, avoid the temptation of a bargain and buy the smaller, more expensive forms.

**Below:** 'Mrs Richardson' really does need a large pond to feel at home. With its 23cm (9in) blooms and wide spreading habit, it will rapidly swamp all but the largest of open water spaces.

# Tropical water lilies

As the number of people in cool temperate climates with conservatories increases, tropical water lilies are becoming more popular. They include a number of species with blue flowers (a colour not present in hardy types) and can be divided into day- and night-blooming varieties. On the whole, these plants have the edge on hardy water lilies right across the board. They are larger, with bigger, often more highly scented flowers, and certainly more profuse. Flower sizes as large as 10in (25cm) are common and some have flowers 12in (30cm) across that are held 12in (30cm) above the surface. These are spectacular plants well worth the trouble needed to keep them.

A pond in a conservatory maintained at a temperature above 18°C (64°F) will suit them well. As with hardy lilies, the plants need to be positioned where they will receive full sun during as much of the day as possible.

For those people who are out at work during most of the day the night-blooming lilies are a very good option. These are highly scented and open their flowers just as the sun is setting. Seen in moonlight, or more reliably by floodlight, the true beauty of these lilies can be appreciated. They close again at around midday, although on cloudy days they may remain open all day.

*Left: 'Mrs George C. Hitchcock' is a vigorous, night-blooming variety that can produce flowers up to 35cm (14in) across. The gorgeous pink flowers are held well above the surface.*

*Left: If you want a blue water lily you will have to grow one of the tropical varieties. 'King of the Blues' is among the best ones to choose. It needs warm conditions and full sunshine if it is to do well in a cool temperate climate.*

*Right: 'H. C. Haarstick' is a night-blooming variety that bears brilliant red flowers up to 30cm (12in) across. This is a reliable plant well worth seeking out from specialist growers.*

**Right:** 'Emily Grant Hutchings' is a very beautiful reddish pink night-blooming variety. Flowers open as the sun sets and may stay open into the next morning on overcast days.

**Below:** 'General Pershing' is probably the best of the pink day-blooming varieties. It has scented double flowers up to 25cm (10in) across. These open as the sun rises and stay open until it sets. It is a common variety on specialist growers lists.

**Above:** 'Mrs Pring' occasionally turns up on specialist water lily lists. It has pale yellow petals and bright golden yellow stamens. A very pretty plant named after a member of the Pring family, responsible for a great deal of work in water lily development.

# Submerged plants

Submerged plants are an essential part of any aquatic ecosystem. They are particularly important in a garden pond because they act as oxygenators and help to keep the water pure and healthy. In ponds with filter systems, the ammonia will be broken down into nitrite and then nitrate by bacteria living on the biological filter media. This leads to a build-up of nitrate, which is not as poisonous as ammonia or nitrite, but is still damaging to fish and aquatic life. Plants use nitrate as food and so remove it from the water. Submerged aquatics are very good at doing this, so some large clumps of these plants should be included in any pond.

While most submerged aquatic plants will only be visible as a green blob beneath the water surface, some do send up stems or flowers above the surface. These make them particularly useful for positioning at the pond edge, where they will help to soften the barrier between the water and the land.

Most submerged plants are sold as a bunch of stem cuttings held together by a lead strip. Remove the lead and plant the cuttings as separate stems into a planting basket full of aquatic potting mixture, as shown here.

*1 Submerged plants will grow much more successfully if you separate out the cuttings and plant them individually.*

*2 Remove the cuttings from their basket and carefully unwrap the packing material and lead strip. Using sharp scissors, trim the base of the stems where they have been crushed by the lead strip. Cut above any damaged areas, leaving only clean, healthy tissue.*

*3 Using a cane, make holes in the aquatic planting mixture at 5cm (2in) intervals. Carefully insert each stem into a hole.*

*4 Backfill with mix and firm each stem into place with your fingers. Cover the surface with a 2.5cm (1in) layer of aquarium gravel.*

*5 Water the pot thoroughly before placing in the pond. The stems will send out side shoots, creating a large mass of oxygenating plants.*

## ▼ Callitriche hermaphroditica
### Autumn starwort

This is probably the best of the oxygenators, yet rarely used in garden ponds. The leaves are small and cresslike in appearance. It is an evergreen and active throughout the winter months. However, growth tends to be more moderate than in some submerged plants and it usually remains low down in the pond, so it is less likely to overcrowd a smaller goldfish pond.

**Environment:** While not the easiest of submerged plants to establish, autumn starwort will thrive in full sun and a mature pond. In new ponds (with less nitrate in the water) there may not be sufficient food available for it to grow well. Fully hardy down to -15°C (5°F).

**Planting depth:** 10-50cm (4-20in)

**Maximum spread:** Indefinite

**Propagation:** Take stem cuttings during spring and summer.

**Winter care:** No special winter care is needed other than to brush snow off any ice that forms on the pond. This allows light to reach the plant so that it can continue to produce oxygen during the day.

## ▲ Ceratophyllum demersum
### Hornwort

This plant is unusual in that it does not root into the substrate, but tends to grow as a free-floating mass of branching stems. These carry tight whorls of bristlelike, light green leaves and are slightly brittle, breaking into small pieces in strong water movement. This allows the plant to disperse far and wide in a pond and form clumps wherever the segments come to rest.

**Environment:** This is a very hardy plant that does well in full sun or deep shade (although growth will be slower in shade).

**Propagation:** Pieces break off by themselves and form new clumps naturally, but you can also take cuttings during the summer.

**Winter care:** In autumn, the stems fall to the bottom of the pond and the plant overwinters as dormant buds.

## ▼ Eleocharis acicularis
### Hairgrass

As its common name suggests, hairgrass looks for all the world like a clump of green hair. It spreads by runners and gradually forms a dense 'lawn'. Depending on the conditions, it can grow 5-25cm (2-10in) tall.

**Environment:** Shorter plants are produced in strong light and cool conditions. Although more often grown as a coldwater aquarium plant, it adapts well to an outdoor pond and will spread a fair distance in one season. Fully hardy down to -15°C (5°F).

**Planting depth:** 10-50cm (4-20in)

**Maximum height:** 25cm (10in)

**Maximum spread:** Indefinite

**Propagation:** Divide the clumps at any time during the growing season.

**Winter care:** No special requirements.

### ▲ Hottonia palustris
Water violet

Few submerged aquatics provide much of a show of flowers, but this one certainly does. Pretty lavender flowers are produced during early summer and rise to about 23cm (9in) above the water surface. The feathery, light green submerged leaves are normally held on thick stems. Water violet spreads slowly to form a sizeable clump, but much of the plant breaks away during late summer and early autumn.

**Environment:** This plant does best in soft, neutral to slightly acidic water. It prefers full sun and a good rich soil to grow in. It can be somewhat tricky to establish and most plants fail during their first winter. If they survive into their second summer, they will usually survive long-term to make a large and very attractive plant. Fully hardy down to -15°C (5°F).

**Planting depth:** 0-60cm (0-24in)

**Maximum spread:** Indefinite

**Propagation:** Cuttings can be taken during summer, but the best way is to plant overwintered turions into new planting baskets in the spring. (Turions are small storage organs complete with roots that develop in clusters on the rootstock.)

**Winter care:** Overwinters in the form of dormant buds. No special winter care needed.

### ▲ Fontinalis antipyretica
Willow moss

This rather unusual-looking plant has dark green, oval leaves borne on very narrow stems. It is an evergreen that will continue to act as an oxygenator, even during the winter. Being slow growing, it is unlikely to cause problems by becoming invasive. Sadly, it is relatively rare in the trade, so few pondkeepers have ever had the chance to include it in their setups.

**Environment:** Unlike most submerged aquatic plants, willow moss likes flowing water, so it can be used at the foot of waterfalls, where few other plants will thrive. Happy in full sun or shade, this adaptable plant is a real asset. Fully hardy down to -15°C (5°F).

**Planting depth:** 10-60cm (4-24in)

**Maximum spread:** Indefinite

**Propagation:** Divide clumps during the growing season or take young shoots as cuttings early in the summer.

**Winter care:** No special requirements.

### ▲ Elodea canadensis
Canadian pondweed

This attractive and very vigorous plant is one of the best submerged oxygenating plants. Dark green leaves are borne in whorls along thin stems that often branch and form large semi-evergreen clumps. It will grow right up to the water surface.

**Environment:** This plant does well in full sun or partial shade. Under no circumstances should it be allowed to grow outside the confines of a container, as it will take over and smother any pond with a mud or soil substrate. Fully hardy down to -15°C (5°F).

**Planting depth:** 10-120cm (4-48in)

**Maximum spread:** Indefinite

**Propagation:** Very easy. Take cuttings throughout the growing season and pot them up in the usual way. New clumps will quickly form.

**Winter care:** No special requirements.

## Lagarosiphon major (Elodea crispa)
Fish weed

The common name tells you all you need to know about this scrambling plant, which has become the most commonly planted oxygenator. Its curved green leaves are set in whorls on branching succulent stems and it is just about evergreen in all but the harshest of winters. Young foliage is paler green in colour.

**Environment:** Be sure to control this vigorous plant by growing it in baskets and never introduce fish weed into a pond with a soil substrate. It thrives in full sun or partial shade, but is prone to become leggy in deep shade. Fully hardy down to -15°C (5°F).

**Planting depth:** 10-120cm (1-18in)

**Maximum spread:** Indefinite

**Propagation:** Cuttings can be taken at any time during the growing season, but since old plants tend to fade and become less vigorous as the years go by, it is a good idea to start new baskets every year and discard half the old plants.

**Winter care:** Cut back by two-thirds in the autumn. No other care is needed.

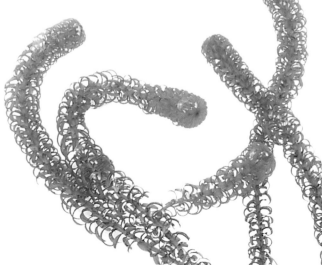

## Myriophyllum aquaticum
Parrot's feather

This very popular aquatic plant has featherlike leaves growing in whorls around a central stem. Underwater, the leaves tend to be much finer and floppy, but above water they are held stiffly away from the stem. The foliage turns red in autumn, before falling off. The main stems tend to meander around underwater, with only the top growth held above the surface, and remain submerged during the winter.

**Environment:** This is a true aquatic plant in that most of it lives underwater. It prefers full sun. It is usually sold in bunches, with several stems held together by a lead strip. Separate the stems and plant several into a basket, leaving at least 5cm (2in) between them. It will tolerate temperatures down to 0°C (32°F). Avoid releasing this rampant plant into natural waterways.

**Planting depth:** 10-60cm (4-24in)

**Maximum height above water:** 10cm (4in)

**Maximum spread:** Indefinite

**Propagation:** Very easy to propagate. Just take cuttings any time during the growing season and plant them into a basket containing aquatic planting mixture.

**Winter care:** As this plant is only half hardy, it is a good idea to collect some stems after leaf fall and keep them in a bucket of water in a cold frame or greenhouse during the cold winter months.

# Submerged plants

## Myriophyllum spicatum
### Spiked milfoil

This pretty plant has long trailing stems and fine, feathery, reddish green submerged foliage. It grows into a large spreading clump and produces red flowers that are held about 2.5cm (1in) above the water surface.

**Environment:** Position the container in an area where it will receive sunshine for at least part of the day, in water up to 90cm (36in) deep. Renew the plants by taking cuttings early in summer every other year. Will tolerate temperatures down to -15°C (5°F).

**Planting depth:** Up to 90cm (36in)

**Maximum spread:** Indefinite

**Propagation:** Take cuttings throughout the growing season.

**Winter care:** No special requirements. Cut back plants by about two-thirds in autumn.

Spiked milfoil is one of the hardier members of the genus and will do well in a wildlife pond.

*Right:* Oxygenating plants such as this whorled water milfoil make massive growth during the summer months but need heavy pruning in the autumn to prevent a build-up of decaying plant matter in winter.

## Myriophyllum verticillatum
### Whorled water milfoil

A rooted submerged plant with light green, needlelike foliage. Branched stems spread out to form a large clump, and in summer small, yellowish green flowers are produced on stems held above the water.

**Environment:** This submerged plant does well in full sun or partial shade. This is an ideal plant for the shallower areas of ponds. Fish will use it for spawning and other wildlife will seek cover in it. It will tolerate temperatures down to -15°C (5°F).

**Planting depth:** 10-45cm (4-18in)

**Maximum height above water:** 15cm (6in)

**Maximum spread:** Indefinite

**Propagation:** Take cuttings throughout the growing season. Establish new baskets every two or three years to keep the plants looking young and fresh.

**Winter care:** No special requirements. During autumn, cut back the stems by about two-thirds. This will encourage new fresh growth the following spring.

## ▶ Ranunculus aquatilis
### Water crowfoot

A wonderful plant for a pond of any size. Not only does it have submerged, oxygenating, threadlike foliage, but it also produces rounded floating leaves that create a carpet on the surface. This provides ideal cover for a whole host of animals. During late spring and early summer, a mass of white-and-yellow flowers appear above the floating foliage. Once these have faded, the surface growth dies back.

**Environment:** Position this plant in a quiet spot near the edge of the pond, where it will thrive in sun or shade. It tolerates some water movement and temperatures down to -15°C (5°F).
**Planting depth:** 10-100cm (4-39in)
**Maximum height above water:** 7.5cm (3in)
**Maximum spread:** Indefinite
**Propagation:** Take cuttings of non-flowering shoots in early summer.
**Winter care:** No special requirements.

## ▲ Potamogeton crispus
### Curled pondweed

This seaweed-like plant is not often offered for sale, yet it is an excellent oxygenator and will not become invasive. The stems bear straplike leaves that are green when grown in shade, but turn bronze or even red in full sun. White flowers tinged with red appear just above the water surface in early summer.
**Environment:** Prefers flowing water, although it will grow in still water. Apart from losing the red tinge to its leaves, it will grow well in full shade as well as in full sun. Will tolerate temperatures down to -15°C (5°F).
**Planting depth:** 10-60cm (4-24in)
**Maximum height above water:** 2.5cm (1in)
**Maximum spread:** Indefinite
**Propagation:** Take cuttings in midsummer.
**Winter care:** No special requirements. Trim back overgrown plants in autumn.

# PLANT INDEX

Page numbers in **bold** indicate major entries; *italics* refer to captions and annotations; plain type indicates other text entries.

## CREDITS

Practical photographs by Geoffrey Rogers © Interpet Publishing.

The publishers would like to thank the following photographers for providing images, credited here by page number and position: B(Bottom), T(Top), C(Centre), BL(Bottom Left), etc.

The Beaver Collection © Sue Westlake-Guy: 27(TR, BR), 31(BC), 32(TL), 43(L), 64(L, R), 65(L), 66(L, R), 67(T, BL), 68(BL), 71(BL), 72(BR), 74(TR)
Dave Bevan: 8(B, TR), 9(L), 13, 18(BR), 20(R), 21(TL, TR, BR), 23(R), 24(C), 35(L), 72(T), 74(BL), 75(L)
Eric Crichton: 17(BR), 18(BC), 29(TR), 30(BL), 31(TL), 32(TR), 38(R), 40(C), 46(C), 47(BL, TC), 51(TC, BR), 53(L, R), 56(C, TR), 57(BR), 73(T), 75(R)
John Glover: 6, 10(TR), 11(L), 14(L), 15(R), 16(BC), 18(BL), 26(TC), 40(R), 45(L), 50(R), 60(C), 69(TR, BR)
Sunniva Harte: 12
S & O Mathews: Copyright page, 8(TC), 15(BL), 17(TR), 18(TR), 34(L), 36(R), 37(R), 46(R), 54(L), 55(B), 57(TL), 60(TR), 61(TL, BR)
Peter J May: 10(BC)
Clive Nichols Garden Pictures: 14(R), 16(L), 31(TR), 43(C), 45(R), 49(BR), 50(L), 51(BL), 52(L), 54(TR), 55(R), 59, 67(BR)
Geoffrey Rogers (Ideas into Print): 20(L), 48(TR), 49(TC, BL)
Neil Sutherland © Geoffrey Rogers: 16(TR), 17(BL), 39(R), 42(C), 65(R), 68(T, BR), 69(L, BR)

Illustrations by Phil Holmes and Stuart Watkinson © Interpet Publishing.

The publishers would like to thank Anglo Aquarium Ltd., Enfield, Middlesex for providing plants and facilities for photography.